Make Just One Change

Make Just One Change

Teach Students to Ask
Their Own Questions

DAN ROTHSTEIN
LUZ SANTANA

GOVERNORS STATE UNIVERSITY
UNIVERSITY PARK, IL

Harvard Education Press
Cambridge, Massachusetts

Library of Congress Control Number 2011928627

Paperback ISBN: 978-1-61250-099-7
Library Edition ISBN: 978-1-61250-100-0

Published by Harvard Education Press,
an imprint of the Harvard Education Publishing Group

Harvard Education Press
8 Story Street
Cambridge, MA 02138

Cover Design: Sarah Henderson
The typefaces used in this book are Minion Pro and Myriad Pro.

*To all the people in communities
across the United States and beyond
from whom we have learned so much
and, going forward, to all those from
whom we expect to learn even more.*

Contents

Foreword

Every generation of Americans has wrestled with the challenge of educating America's children. By now, most Americans acknowledge the need to educate all children to a high standard. Given the social, political, and economic pressures such as globalization, rapidly changing demographics, immigration, and the interplay between domestic and international policy, our students must now more than ever grasp high levels of knowledge and skills to gain entry into the full economic and civic benefits of our democratic way of life.

In my work with citizens around the country who are laboring to improve education for all children, I see a hunger for two things: an inspiring, bold vision of schools where children flourish, and practical tools that can help make that possible. That's a difficult combination to come by.

In *Make Just One Change*, Dan Rothstein and Luz Santana provide us with a rare example of that combination—an inspiring vision of education at its best and an extraordinarily clear, low-tech, practical intellectual tool for turning that vision into reality. Their basic argument is very simple: we should be teaching the skill of question formulation to all students. We should do it to promote excellence and we should do it to promote equity. Both are achievable.

This point seems almost too obvious. The skill of question formulation—a thinking ability with universal relevance—can make all learning possible. In the many examples presented in these pages, the authors show how the ability to ask questions also leads to new ideas, new inventions, and better solutions. We can also see that learning how to ask questions also leads to improved learning outcomes, greater student engagement, and more ownership of the learning process. This book asks teachers to make one simple change in their regular practice; to deliberately teach students how to ask their own questions. Perhaps its greatest contribution is that it takes this challenging idea and shows not only *why* it should be done but exactly *how* it can be done. It offers a step-by-step process—the Question Formulation Technique—that has been developed through years of testing, practice and refinement.

The examples in *Make Just One Change* can help us understand how schools can increase student achievement, build new relationships between learner and teacher, and open new avenues for dialogue and inquiry. It can give us hope that what happens in a classroom where students are learning to ask questions can truly be a building block for creating productive relationships that benefit our entire society and our democracy.

It is not surprising that the Right Question Institute created this new technique. The authors, with their combination of complementary skills, experiences and perspectives, have been tilling this field of improving education and society by working with parents, students, teachers, and community residents around the country for the past two decades. Rothstein has a doctorate in education from Harvard, but has committed himself to learning from people far from power and with limited education. Santana, who travelled a path that included emigrating from Puerto Rico to moving from being a welfare recipient to working on a factory floor to getting a master's degree, has committed herself to teaching others how to help themselves instead of becoming the spokesperson on their behalf. This book is not their first breakthrough, but is a landmark—a bringing together of years of research and experience into a methodology for applying their groundbreaking thought and technique.

There are several reasons to read this book. One is it so strongly inspires hope—something desperately needed in a world where we face so many overwhelming challenges. Hope is what keeps us looking for ways to solve these challenges—to bring about peace in the world or to end the stranglehold of poverty. We hope to find a new path, a Northwest passage, another way to solve a problem. I would posit that hope lives in the mind and grows in thoughtful dialogue with itself and others. And that sometimes springs from figuring out what questions we need to ask. This book, therefore, gives us a way not only for students to learn how to generate questions, but also, in the process, gives us hope and strength for moving forward in the hard work of making education work better for all students. All students will benefit, including those who already excel at answering questions, but not necessarily asking them.

Beyond helping those who are currently deemed successful, the Question Formulation Technique is a powerful tool that addresses the urgent need to improve education for students in struggling schools and districts. We must invest in the capacity of all students to think more clearly and more deeply, to learn more, and to feel greater ownership of their own learning. These are the skills and habits of mind of successful learners and they should not be restricted to students in elite institutions. This book can help make the case that deliberately teaching the skill of question formulation can also lead to the goal of greater academic achievement as set by the Common Core State Standards.

Make Just One Change allows students to discover just how powerful it is to ask questions as a way to guide their own learning. The inspiring examples of students and teachers in this book push me to ask my own questions: *Why* wouldn't *we teach an essential, powerful, important, and robust skill to all students? Why would we want to keep it from them?* The strength of the nation is tied to the intellectual competency and capacity of our people. If we commit to a vision of all students learning to ask their own questions, and, by doing so, becoming more self-directed and successful learners, we now have a book that shows us how to turn that vision into reality.

Wendy D. Puriefoy
President
Public Education Network

"Why Didn't I Learn This in School?"

This book makes two simple arguments:

- All students should learn how to formulate their own questions.
- All teachers can easily teach this skill as part of their regular practice.

The inspiration for the first argument came from an unusual source. Parents in the low-income community of Lawrence, Massachusetts, with whom we were working twenty years ago told us that they did not participate in their children's education nor go to their children's schools because they "didn't even know what to ask."

It turns out that they were actually pointing to a glaring omission in most formal and informal educational enterprises. The skill of being able to generate a wide range of questions and strategize about how to use them effectively is rarely, if ever, deliberately taught. In fact, it has too often been limited to students who have access to an elite education. Our goal is to democratize the teaching of an essential thinking and learning skill that is also an essential democratic skill.

The parents who named the problem so clearly started us on a long journey. They clarified for us that there is no one set of "right questions," but rather, that everyone needs the opportunity to figure out the questions that are right for them to ask. We eventually learned, through much trial and error, how to teach what turns out to be a very sophisticated, higher-order thinking skill to people of all educational and income levels—an educational strategy that is now used across a range of fields. We also saw that people can get better at asking questions, generate more productive questions, and then figure out just the right questions for them to be asking if they have the opportunity to develop their own ability to ask questions. In just the past few years, we have begun to share the strategy with classroom teachers in different parts of the country.

Our second argument is actually inspired by those very teachers and their students from a wide range of schools. They have successfully demonstrated that teaching the skill of question formulation can be part of ordinary classroom practice. It becomes a familiar way of thinking and learning that produces transformational moments of new discovery and greater ownership by students of their own learning.

The students you will hear from in this book are a remarkably diverse group, representing different ages, backgrounds, and levels of academic success. Some live in suburban communities with parents who are university faculty or software engineers, some live with their families in densely populated urban neighborhoods, and some are even living on their own and working as well as going to school. No matter what their background and socioeconomic status may be, all of these students share common discoveries about the power of generating questions and the relevance of this skill to their lives and studies.

The teachers also represent a wide range of backgrounds. Some have decades of experience and some are in their very first years of teaching, but veterans and novices alike have integrated a deceptively simple protocol—the *Question Formulation Technique* (QFT™)—into their classroom practice. In this book, we will offer examples of how teachers used the protocol with students in different subjects, grade levels, and schools. They share their excitement and sometimes their surprise at how teaching the skill helps them achieve their teaching goals more quickly and efficiently. They also express deep satisfaction as they see their students rapidly develop divergent, convergent, and metacognitive thinking abilities and become more confident learners.

WHAT HAPPENS WHEN STUDENTS LEARN TO ASK QUESTIONS?

Ling-Se Peet, a high school humanities teacher with three years of experience in the Boston public schools system, shared with us her experience teaching a ninth-grade summer school class: fourteen- to-fifteen-year olds who, with an F+ for the year, had just missed the cutoff for advancing to tenth grade in the fall.[1] Whatever their reasons for being there—illness, family crisis, or just plain struggling with lessons and homework—her job was to get them back on track so they could advance with the rest of their class.

During the first week of the program, Peet pushed and cajoled the class through a rigorous process of question-asking related to a reading assignment. Those hot

July mornings, the students were prodded to think harder than many could ever recall doing. There were definitely some signs of interest and engagement, but there was also another, more pained look in evidence, expressed best by a gangly fifteen-year old who waved his arm slowly from side to side: "Miss Peet! Miss Peet!" It took a few calls, but finally he got her attention: "Miss Peet, my brain is hurtin' from asking all these questions."

Peet had indeed put a big hurt on her students that day. Offering just a few clear instructions, she had taken them through a demanding process in which they learned how to produce their own questions, improve these questions, prioritize them, and lay out some next steps for how they would be used.

Nine full years into their formal education, these youths had never done anything like the QFT and, though they found it taxing, they also found it challenging and stimulating. They climbed a sharp learning curve pretty quickly, and apparently that made an impression on them. Rosa, whose attention on other days had been entirely on her pocket mirror, wrote at the end of the class that she "felt *smart* asking all these questions"—a term that had not previously been part of her lexicon when describing her experience at school.

The kinds of changes noted by Peet's students also show up in communities where students consistently do well in school. A librarian at the J. L. Stanford Middle School, a public school in Palo Alto, California, observed some of those changes. She noticed that students in Hayley Dupuy's science class and Katie Schramm's social studies class had clearly benefited from learning how to come up with their own questions. "Your students," she told them, "are very well prepared to do research and work on their own as independent learners."

Dupuy and Schramm, dedicated, resourceful veteran teachers with a combined twenty-one years of classroom experience, had recently started to explicitly teach students how to formulate their own questions. They, their students, and even some of the students' parents noticed the difference. One parent told Dupuy: "I see the difference in my younger son. Learning how to ask his own questions put him further ahead in his project work than I saw with his older siblings."

The rigorous process of learning to develop and ask questions offers students the invaluable opportunity to become independent thinkers and self-directed learners. Many teachers who aspire to do precisely that often struggle against significant odds—overcrowded classrooms, underresourced schools, demanding directives from central office, and students who seem either too harried or too alienated to engage seriously with the life of the classroom. Yet the teachers with whom we have worked find that using the QFT *actually lightens their load*, while leading to better outcomes and greater student ownership of learning.[2]

THE QUESTION FORMULATION TECHNIQUE

The Question Formulation Technique has been painstakingly developed, tested, simplified, and improved over the past two decades. The protocol has six core components:

- A *Question Focus*, usually developed by the teacher that serves as the jumping-off point for student questions.
- A process for students to *produce questions* using a set of four simple rules
- An exercise for students to work on *closed- and open-ended questions*
- Student *selection of priority questions*
- A teacher and student plan for *next steps*—how they will use the priority questions
- A *reflection* activity for students to name what they have learned, how they learned it, and how they will use what they have learned

The QFT offers a very straightforward, step-by-step, rigorous process that mixes easily with *your* explicit and implicit teaching knowledge. We call the book *Make Just One Change* because 90 percent of what is involved in using the QFT allows you to continue doing what you already do as a teacher: design a lesson plan; create activities to help students learn new material; guide individual, small group, and whole class learning activities; troubleshoot problems in the learning process; and facilitate discussions.

There is but one change being asked of you in this book: you will be leading a process in which your students will be thinking and working by asking their *own* questions, rather than by responding to questions *you* ask. This may feel strange at first—for both you and your students. It does not replace everything you do, it simply adds one new element to your teaching. Once the QFT becomes part of your practice and that of your students, it becomes a renewable resource in your teaching repertoire and in their learning repertoire.

Make Just One Change will show how the process is used in a wide range of communities and schools, with students of all ages and levels of academic readiness. There are examples of individual teachers using the QFT in their own classrooms and of teachers working together to build and reinforce the skill of question asking across different subject areas and for different purposes within schools. The students deploy their new skills to help them write essays, read challenging texts, identify and refine research questions, design experiments, unpack mathematical formulas, plan Socratic seminars, and even create homework assignments for themselves.[3] Through these examples you can quickly see how to easily use the QFT to strengthen and enrich your lesson plans and attain your most ambitious teaching and curricular goals.

Origins of the Question Formulation Technique

Our vision and practice was shaped not only by the voices in this book, but also by years of experience working as educators in many communities. The QFT did not develop in a school-based research project, a university seminar, or a think tank. We garnered the original insight about the importance of the skill of question formulation from the parents in that low-income community in Massachusetts with which we opened this introduction. One of us (Luz Santana) knew well from her own experience as a welfare recipient the kinds of challenges the parents were facing when trying to navigate their way through complicated systems. One of us (Dan Rothstein) had worked on a range of community and municipal efforts to make it possible for people who have often been ignored to have a voice in decisions that affect them.

In the late 1980s, we were working as part of a dropout prevention program funded by the Annie E. Casey Foundation. It was during that project that we heard from parents, repeatedly, that despite their worries about their children's education, they would not come to meetings at the school because they "didn't even know what to ask." We were very smart—it only took us one or two . . . thousand times of hearing that statement to realize that maybe they had something there. And then, of course, we immediately went out and "solved" that problem by giving them questions to ask. If they had a concern one week about a referral to special education, we gave them questions for that. If the issue changed the next week, for example, to report cards, or disciplinary policies, or graduation requirements, they kept returning to be given a new set of questions.

But this was exactly the *wrong* thing to do. Providing parents with the questions in situation after situation did nothing to build their capacity or confidence that they could ever figure out for themselves how to advocate more effectively for their children, partner more productively with school staff, or clarify what they wanted and needed to know, whatever the topic or situation. It only fostered greater dependency.

We eventually understood that the problem the parents had named was not about the need for specific questions but more about *the need to know how to generate and use their own questions*. It seems obvious in hindsight, but the problem had never before been named so clearly. The insight was significant, but we were still left with this challenge: how do you teach the skill of question formulation to people who have not had access to higher education, many of whom have not finished high school, and some of whom have low literacy levels and language barriers to overcome?

We started right then on a twenty-year journey that has led us to an unexpected area of expertise—and we use *expertise* as defined by the Nobel Prize–winning physicist Niels Bohr: "An expert is someone who has made all possible mistakes in one field and there are no more to make." We have, indeed, learned through a long process of making many mistakes and learning from them exactly how to teach people with limited education and income sophisticated skills of thinking and expression. We were part of a core group that created The Right Question Project, now known as The Right Question Institute, for the primary purpose of teaching what we had learned to people working in many fields and many communities across this country and beyond.[4]

Our work with The Right Question Institute kept leading us to discoveries of both the depth of the challenges people face and the need to create simple and effective methods for teaching essential thinking and self-advocacy skills. We created the Right Question Strategy to teach two core skills: the ability to ask questions and the ability to participate effectively in decisions. We saw sugarcane plantation workers in Hawaii, about to lose their livelihoods, learn to focus on key decisions and ask questions about how they could secure economic development opportunities for microenterprise and secure homes and services to replace what had previously been company-provided health care and housing. We saw welfare recipients in rural Northern California learn to advocate for better job training to move off welfare. We saw immigrant parents on the New Mexico–Mexico border cross the school threshold for the first time after a shooting in a middle school and press for violence prevention activities.

We also learned a great deal from the use of our strategy in health-care research projects led by medical school faculty members in Boston and New York. Their work showed that as patients in low-income communities learned to ask questions about their care, they began to partner more effectively with health-care providers. Those projects led to articles in the medical literature demonstrating how the Right Question Strategy leads to significant increases in patient activation.[5]

Discovering the Value of the Question Formulation Technique for Adult Literacy Programs

In the late 1990s, we began to learn more about the value of our methods in a classroom environment—as a teaching practice—when Art Ellison and Patricia Nelson of the New Hampshire Bureau of Adult Education brought The Right Question Strategy into adult literacy, GED, and ESOL programs across the state. Instructors reported that as adult learners learned to ask their own questions, they became more confident learners in the classroom. The adult literacy and GED students, none of whom had completed high school, impressed themselves as well as their teachers with their newfound ability to comprehend more, write and read better, and take more responsibility for their own learning. One adult literacy student told his instructor: "This work, asking questions, is hard work. I've had to do more thinking than I've ever done." Then he paused and asked: "Can we do this again tomorrow?"

Adult educators, accustomed to working with a young adult population that has never had success in school and often struggles with very basic learning tasks, comment on the profound changes they see in students who learn to ask questions. A veteran teacher who taught the QFT in her GED class noted, "My students were so struck by the way learning how to formulate their own questions helped them learn. They wondered, 'Why didn't I learn this in high school?'"[6]

It was a good question, and it definitely pushed us to think about how to encourage more teachers to use the strategy. We focused first on expanding implementation in adult literacy programs in other New England states and then in other parts of the country. Donald Green and Shang Ha at Yale's Institution for Social and Policy Studies led a research project examining how the RQP Strategy in adult literacy classrooms helped students think more about active citizen participation and voting. A participant in a program in central Pennsylvania that was part of the study drew this conclusion: "Learning how to ask questions is the most important thing I've ever learned. It helps me learn."

We also discovered how little the students in many of the adult literacy programs were participating in decisions in their ordinary encounters with public institutions. We realized that if they were not participating on this micro level, it did not seem reasonable to expect that they would act on the macro level of democracy—for example, in the voting booth, city council meetings, communicating with elected officials, or organizing or lobbying for policy changes. We worked with Agnes S. Bain of Suffolk University to develop the concept of *microdemocracy* to draw attention to how people can begin to participate effectively in decisions that directly affect them. They can take the first steps of democratic action by learning and using self-advocacy skills—asking questions and participating in decisions—that are also essential democratic skills. Once they do that, their individual encounters can become a new gateway to other forms of democratic action. The Right Question Institute continues to work on microdemocracy in many fields and communities.

Extending the Question Formulation Technique to K–12 Education

Professor Richard Murnane of the Harvard Graduate School of Education, in his work with the Boston public school system, introduced The Right Question Strategy to teachers, principals, and administrators as a resource for analyzing student achievement data in order to improve classroom practices and better address student needs.[7] This work on school improvement and our experiences in adult literacy programs prodded us to examine how to share the strategy more directly with teachers in K–12 classrooms.

In 2003, we were invited to give an Askwith Lecture at the Harvard Graduate School of Education to introduce our strategy to more educators. One of the participants wrote after the talk: "Why don't more people know about this? It boggles the mind." This anonymous respondent's reaction was similar to that of the parents in Lawrence years before. It had become obvious that the QFT should be taught in the K–12 environment and that we needed to provide the strategy to more educators. We began to introduce the QFT to teachers at national conferences and were impressed by how eager they were to learn it and how quickly they began to use it in their classrooms.

Teachers learning the strategy for the first time were often struck by the deceptively simple change of getting students to ask their own questions. Laurie Gaughran, a veteran history teacher at New York City's Humanities Preparatory Academy ("Humanities Prep") observed:

> I see that [knowing how to ask questions] is what I'd like my students to do but I never had a process for doing it. I also think about how when they submit a paper to me and I want them to think more about it, I go ahead and list all kinds of questions—writing on the margins of their papers—to get them to think about it all. But the QFT is pushing me to see that it would be better if they could look at their own work and learn to ask the kinds of questions I'm asking and some I am not thinking about.

Gaughran's discovery is representative of many teachers' responses when they realize that the QFT is about making one small but quite significant and meaningful shift. They begin to imagine the questions appearing not as teacher suggestions in the margins, but as students' own creations that guide and prod them to figure out things on their own. A high school teacher in Maryland noted that the QFT "empowers students to be responsible for their own learning and also helps them refine a skill that has direct practical function and application in their daily lives."

Another high school teacher in Portland, Oregon, described overcoming skepticism from colleagues who "did not think students would be able to produce their own questions." After she implemented the process in her classes [and it helped shape twelve weeks of student work that followed] her colleagues realized that "they were wrong . . . Now, they are inspired to get *their* kids to ask questions."

In the process of collecting evidence in preparation for writing this book, we had a special opportunity to work with teachers working in a range of classroom and school environments with very different student populations. Teachers in elementary school classrooms have effectively used the QFT with their students, but in the chapters that follow you will hear primarily from middle and high school teachers who are successfully teaching their students how to formulate their own questions. In the past year, we've also had the chance to work closely with the Boston Day and Evening Academy (BDEA), a public high school with a population of students who have transferred from or aged out of other high schools in the city. These youth face a range of difficulties, and keeping them engaged and motivated is a constant challenge for their teachers. The teachers who have used the QFT in their classrooms have reported that the process leads to students who take far more ownership of their own learning than they have ever seen. "They're motivated to find out the answers to their own questions," Marcy Ostberg, a science teacher, reports. She observed that when her students were working on a unit on the evolution of the eye, they not only "took ownership of their research and designed experiments and wrote research papers [but also acquired a] language and understanding of questions" that allowed them "to come up with a more thorough research question and subsequent questions." Her teaching became easier because as students became less dependent on her, she could do more work with individuals to help them "push their thinking deeper."

Many of the students at the BDEA have become accustomed to teachers across different classrooms and disciplines who use the QFT. One student who was struggling through family crises and frequent moves as she tried to make it through high school knew that she'd be pushed to think for herself and ask her own questions in yet another class at the school. In her humanities classes, she voiced her feeling to teachers Yana Minchenko and Rachel Jean-Marie that she didn't always like having to do that much thinking, but then articulated, about as succinctly as possible, why it is worth doing. "You need to learn to do it, because when teachers tell you what to think, you don't learn *nothing*."

For more perspectives on the value of knowing how to ask questions, see "The Importance of Asking Questions."

Our work in education over the past few years has shaped the structure of this book to ensure that it is helpful to the wide population of teachers who want to teach the skill to their students.

THE STRUCTURE OF THE BOOK

In chapter 1, we discuss how the Question Formulation Technique manages in one process to actually develop multiple thinking abilities and learning skills. We provide a brief overview of what you and your students will do in each step of the QFT, show how the steps relate to specific thinking abilities, and examine the parts of the

QFT that rely on the "art" of teaching and the parts that offer a "science"—a protocol and specific rules that produce replicable results.

In chapters 2 through 8, with the help of teachers and students in classrooms in various locations around the country, we take you through each aspect of the QFT. Each chapter is structured to provide you with an overview of the particular step, examples of how it is used with students, and troubleshooting advice on how to use the step in your own classroom.

In chapter 2, you will see the similarities and differences between a traditional prompt and a *Question Focus* (or *QFocus*) for stimulating student questions. We will share examples of how teachers design their QFocus by keeping in mind the lesson and curricular goals they have set for their students. In chapter 3, we present four *Rules for Producing Questions* that make it possible for students, even those who have never before done so, to generate their own questions. We take apart each rule in depth, detailing its function as one of the four legs necessary to make the "table" of question formation stand on its own. Chapter 4 provides a window into a few examples of what happens when students in different schools and age groups and subjects start to produce their own questions.

Chapter 5 discusses the importance of *closed- and open-ended questions* and how students learn to change their questions from one category to the other as needed. Chapter 6 offers a view into how students in different classes *prioritize* their questions and the thinking that accompanies the prioritization process. Chapter 7 provides examples of how student questions are used to move ahead toward specific teaching and learning outcomes. The chapter presents examples of the many ways teachers and students can use student questions for both immediate tasks and long-term projects. Chapter 8 concludes the unpacking of the QFT by looking at the final step, *reflection*, which offers students the opportunity to reinforce their experience of the earlier steps by naming what they learned, how they learned, and how they can use this learning—now and in the future.

Chapter 9 offers a composite, in memo form, of advice that teachers may pass on to each other about how to teach students to ask their own questions and the surprises and challenges they'll encounter when using the QFT in their classrooms. In chapter 10, we analyze and categorize the changes the QFT produces in students as well as in classroom practice. We also share what we have learned from many teachers in low-income communities who have discovered that the QFT is a very effective

---

The Importance of Asking Questions

Is teaching students how to ask their own questions really so important? Here are just a few of a great many observations that make the case for the importance of questions:

Young children: "Children are natural question-askers. They have to be to learn how to adapt to a complex and changing environment. But whether they continue to ask questions . . . depends in large part on how adults respond to them." (Robert Sternberg)[a]

Students in grade and high school: "[A]ll the knowledge we have is a result of our asking questions; indeed . . . question-asking is the most significant intellectual tool human beings have. Is it not curious, then, that the most significant intellectual skill available to human beings is not taught in school? I can't resist repeating that: The most significant intellectual skill available to human beings I not taught in school." (Neal Postman)[b]

College students: In 2002, the *New York Times* asked several college presidents what students should learn from four years of college. Leon Botstein, the president of Bard College, responded, "The primary skills should be analytical skills of interpretation and inquiry. In other words, to know how to frame a question." Nancy Cantor, current president of Syracuse University, said that the world is so complicated that "the best we can do for students is to have them ask the right questions." (Kate Zernike)[c]

---

tool for improving educational outcomes for disadvantaged students. We conclude with a vision or just how much could be accomplished if every student mastered the QFT: when students learn to ask their own questions, they can immediately become better learners and, in the long run, become effective contributors to building a strong economy and a more thoughtful and engaged democratic citizenry.[8]

MAKING JUST ONE CHANGE—AND MAKING A HUGE DIFFERENCE

Thanks to the initiative of the leadership at the Boston Day and Evening Academy and a number of its teachers, many students are learning how to think for themselves, take more ownership of their own learning, and become more successful

Intellectual labor and genius: "It is left to the greatest scientists to pose questions that no one has posed before, and then to arrive at an answer that changes for all time the way in which scientists (and eventually laymen) construe the universe. Einstein's genius lay in his persistent questioning of the absoluteness of time and space." (Howard Gardner)[d]

Business leadership: "The most common source of management mistakes is not the failure to find the right answers. It is the failure to ask the right questions." (Peter Drucker)[e]

Health care: "A patient is not a doctor [and] lacks a doctor's training and experience. And many laymen feel inhibited about asking questions. But the questions are perfectly legitimate. Patients can learn to question and to think the way a doctor should." (Jerome Groopman)[f]

a. Robert J. Sternberg, "Answering Questions and Questioning Answers: Guiding Children to Intellectual Excellence," *Phi Delta Kappan* 76, no. 2 (1994), http://www.jstor.org/.

b. Neil Postman, *Building a Bridge to the 18th Century: How the Past Can Improve Our Future* (New York: Random House, 1999), 171.

c. Kate Zernike, "Tests Are Not Just for Kids." *New York Times,* August 4, 2002.

d. Howard Gardner, *Frames of Mind: the Theory of Multiple Intelligences* (New York: Basic Books, 1993), 149.

e. Peter Drucker, *The Practice of Management* (1954) 1.

f. Jerome Groopman, *How Doctors Think* (Boston: Houghton Mifflin, 2008), 23.

students. Unlike the the New Hampshire GED student quoted above, they won't have to ask: "Why didn't I learn this in high school?" The high school teachers you'll hear from in this book are making sure their students leave high school equipped with the skill that some college presidents suggest would only be learned through four years of college (see "The Importance of Asking Questions"). In Laurie Gaughran's high school history class, for example, students talked about how they "learned that asking questions is such a simple thing but, at the same time, can open up toward so much opportunity to learn" and that "asking questions has taught me to think in more depth."

Their comments echo those made by Hayley Dupuy and Katie Schramm's students. These teachers are making sure that their students are not leaving the sixth grade without knowing how to ask their own questions. A year after one class, several students came back to Dupuy's classroom and waxed poetic about what they had learned from her and what it meant to them. One seventh-grader described the effect it had on her: "The questions give you boundaries and then let you explore all the way to new boundaries and then they keep you focused on where you need to be." One of her classmates said he felt that knowing how to produce his own questions influenced how he felt about learning and studying: "It makes you more interested and opens whole doors you otherwise would not go through."

We invite you to join the teachers you will hear from in this book who are making it possible for their students to learn how to open many doors for themselves. They will push forward to new intellectual boundaries as they break new ground in their own thinking and in their contributions to the classroom and to society. Your students, whether they have previously experienced academic success or failure, can do amazing things with a rigorous, disciplined, finely honed skill for asking questions.

They won't use what they learned just one time in your classroom. They will carry their ability forward and will be able to ask their own questions wherever they go in their schooling and work, in class and in life. They will be better equipped to become successful, self-directed, lifelong learners. We can look forward to what we learn from them as they carry on researching, creating, building, problem solving, and thinking of timeless questions that still need to be answered and new questions that have yet to be asked.

CHAPTER 1

The Question Formulation Technique

Teaching Multiple Thinking Abilities in One Process

*"I learned that when you ask your own questions
you can actually learn more."*

THE QUESTION FORMULATION TECHNIQUE (QFT) is a step-by-step process designed to facilitate the asking of many questions. But it does more than that—it takes students through a rigorous process in which they think more deeply about their questions, refine them, and prioritize their use. As the students go through the steps of the QFT, they practice, in addition to question formulation, three fundamentally important thinking abilities: divergent thinking, convergent thinking, and metacognition.[1]

In this chapter, we will briefly look at these three thinking abilities and then at their connection to specific steps of the QFT. We will also look at how the QFT is both an *art*—an open process that is continuously shaped by the actions and thoughts of teachers and students—and a *science*—a rigorous, laboratory-tested, scaffolded procedure; a protocol for consistently producing similar, replicable results each time it is deployed.

THREE WISE THINKING ABILITIES

Imagine your students:

- Freely generating new ideas
- Analyzing text

- Synthesizing research
- Making meaning of what they are studying
- Naming what they know and how they can use what they know

In order to do all of the above, they need three distinct thinking abilities:

- **Divergent thinking:** The ability to generate a wide range of ideas and think broadly and creatively
- **Convergent thinking:** The ability to analyze and synthesize information and ideas while moving toward an answer or conclusion
- **Metacognition:** The ability to think about one's own thinking and learning

Each ability on its own is a valuable resource for any student. When put together, their individual potency is multiplied many times over. Let's look for a moment at each one. Then we'll see how they are brought together in the Question Formulation Technique.

Divergent Thinking: Opening the Mind to New Possibilities

Divergent thinking reflects an ability to generate a wide range of ideas, options, hypotheses, and possibilities.[2] It is what your students need to be able to do when they say "I'm stuck" or can't generate ideas about possible research topics or shy away from thinking creatively. They seem to grow less and less comfortable doing divergent thinking the more years they spend in school.

"Creative souls" such as artists, writers, and musicians are respected for their divergent thinking ability, for the way they think out of the box to conjure up unconventional, inventive new ideas. Divergent thinking is almost always seen as a gift rather than an acquired and developed skill. But this view is far from the truth: divergent thinking is a distinct form of higher-order thinking that can be taught to all ages and all students. Research has demonstrated that kindergarteners who practiced divergent thinking showed gains in their abilities, and older students with low academic performance showed an ability to learn divergent thinking and gained greater self-confidence in their overall abilities the more they practiced.[3] When students use divergent thinking, they improve and demonstrate an enhanced ability to generate more ideas and greater flexibility of thought.[4] Perhaps most importantly, the benefits carry forward: students with greater divergent thinking skills show increased confidence in their ability to handle challenges and handle stress better, and they tend to carry this thinking skill into real-world situations.[5]

Convergent Thinking: Synthesis, Analysis, and Making Meaning

The need to promote divergent thinking is not just as an intellectual aspiration, but also a powerful resource for generating new ideas for business and commerce (think about the creative world of the Web 2.0 and social media). There are, however, concerns that creativity—the expected outcome of divergent thinking—is in decline across the country. *Newsweek* dedicated a cover story in 2010 to the "Creativity Crisis"; the article pointed to school-based programs and researchers who demonstrate that creativity requires *convergent* as well as divergent thinking.[6]

Convergent thinking involves the synthesizing of a range of ideas, allowing students to take a collection of facts and examples and make sense of it all. This type of thinking occurs when a student explains, interprets, summarizes, compares, and contrasts—all forms of intellectual activity aimed at pulling things together.[7]

Genuine creativity, the research suggests, "requires constant shifting, blending pulses of both divergent thinking and convergent thinking, to combine new information with old and forgotten ideas. Highly creative people are very good at marshaling their brains" to tap into both kinds of thinking. For schools, it turns out that programs that succeed at fostering creativity in students actually "alternate maximum divergent thinking with bouts of intense convergent thinking."[8]

Metacognition: Learning to Think About Thinking

Although combining divergent and convergent thinking abilities is a potent resource for your students, we need to add one more ability to the mix—*metacognition*, the ability to think about one's own learning and thinking processes. It is a concept with ancient roots, but has recently been shown to be essential for improving the education of all students. The late Ann Brown, a development psychologist and a prominent researcher of metacognition, noted how successful students naturally raise questions about the material they read, make predictions, reflect on the sense and meaning of the story, and wonder and question further about what is happening. She noticed that students who struggle do not apply these methods as they read. She set out with colleagues, including her husband Joseph Campione, to create a strategy to instill such patterns of thinking in these struggling students.

Her idea was to create a "community of learners" in elementary school classrooms that would emphasize these reflective and inquisitive methods in their studies.[9]

Brown, the first member of her family to attend college, learned to read fluently only when she was thirteen. Acutely aware of the need to know how to learn, she argued that "effective learners operate best when they have insight into their own strengths and weaknesses and access to their own repertoires of strategies for learning."[10] Her work focused on the importance of how metacognition allowed learners to understand what they have learned, name how they have learned it, and consider how they can use it in other situations.

The National Research Council report *How People Learn: Brain, Mind, Experience, and School* recognized metacognition as a key factor in learning, and one that needs to be systematically and deliberately developed in all students.[11] The committee members highlighted the particularly important role that metacognition plays in promoting transfer of learning. Students who are aware of themselves as learners and who can name and monitor their own learning strategies can more easily apply knowledge obtained in one context to another.[12]

Most students do not arrive in the classroom equipped with metacognitive skills, nor do they leave with them at the end of their high school years. The problem persists into higher education; research shows that many college students lack basic metacognitive skills and habits to assess their own understanding of content and material.[13] Limited metacognitive abilities can result in inadequate grasp of content, inefficient use of time and attention, overconfidence in one's knowledge, and few attempts to learn from new or contradictory information.[14]

Metacognition, as the National Research Council argued, needs to be deliberately nurtured, as does the ability to think divergently and convergently.[15] They are three extraordinarily important thinking abilities that may not be evident now in your students, but are within their reach. We are about to show you how all three can be nurtured, developed, and mastered in one concise process.

THE QUESTION FORMULATION TECHNIQUE

The Question Formulation Technique (QFT) offers a process and structure within which students can, in a limited amount of time, develop all three abilities and also help them deepen their own understanding of core content and curricular materials. It also fosters their ability to produce their own questions and improve and prioritize them. This chapter's appendix provides a reference card for this process.

As we noted in the introduction, using the QFT requires one small, but significant shift in practice. You will not be asking the questions. Instead, students will be asking all the questions, and you will be facilitating that process. The first time you use this technique in the classroom, you may want to budget a minimum of forty-five minutes for the full process. As you and your students gain more experience, you'll find that you can run through the QFT very quickly, in ten to fifteen minutes, even when students are working in groups. There may also be times when your students will want to use the process alone or you will require that they work on their own.

Table 1.1 shows the QFT steps, teacher and student roles in each step, and the thinking abilities students develop. We will now look briefly at each of the steps (these will be described in full in the following chapters and focus on the specific thinking abilities they foster.

The first step in the QFT is developing and choosing the *Question Focus*, or *QFocus*. This is a stimulus that can come in the form of a statement, a visual or aural aid; anything that can sharply focus and attract the student attention and will stimulate them to formulate their own questions. It is designed to first facilitate students' divergent thinking, but is also designed with the teacher's end goals in mind so that students will need to practice convergent thinking as well. The QFocus is similar to a prompt, with one important difference: it is not a teacher's question but rather the focus for student questions. Chapter 2 will discuss in detail how to design a QFocus and will provide examples of how teachers have designed and used them effectively.

In the second step, four *Rules for Producing Questions* offer a rigorous structure—a protocol—within which students can produce their own questions. The rules set up the process for students to work on their own without assistance from the teacher:

1. Ask as many questions as you can.
2. Do not stop to discuss, judge, or answer any of the questions.
3. Write down every question exactly as it was stated.
4. Change any statements into questions.

TABLE 1.1

The Right Question Institute's Question Formulation Technique

	Teacher role	*Student role*	*Student thinking abilities*
The Question Focus	Set goals for use of the QFT and develop a QFocus.	N/A	N/A
Rules for Producing Questions	Introduce Rules for Producing Questions; facilitate discussions.	Discuss challenges in using the Rules for Producing Questions.	**Metacognitive:** Think and hear from each other about the challenge of "thinking in questions."
Categorizing open- and closed-ended questions	Give instructions to start process; monitor and support student use of the Rules for Producing Questions.	Work in small groups to ask questions related to the QFocus.	**Divergent:** Produce their own questions by following the Rules for Producing Questions.
Improving the questions	Facilitate discussion about open- and closed-ended questions.	Discuss advantages and disadvantages of open- and closed-ended questions; practice changing questions from one type to another.	**Metacognitive:** Think about purpose and use of different kinds of questions for securing information. **Convergent:** Practice changing questions to sharpen scope of inquiry.
Prioritizing the questions	Provide instructions on how to prioritize the questions. Monitor and support student prioritization.	Discuss, compare, assess, and prioritize questions. Select three priority questions and explain choices.	**Convergent:** Analyze, compare, and assess all questions and select three as focus for next steps.
Next steps	Provide direction for using the questions.	Use the questions for purposes set by the teacher.	**Convergent:** Use the questions for specific purposes and learning goals.
Reflection	Facilitate the reflection process.	Discuss what was learned, how it was learned, and what they now know or feel differently about.	**Metacognitive and convergent:** Thinking about the thinking and learning process and about where they are now compared with where they were when they began.

The teacher introduces the rules and asks the students to think about and discuss possible challenges in following them.

The rules ask for a change in behavior, officially discouraging discussion in order to encourage the rapid production of questions. Students thus need to think about how they usually work individually and in groups. They name their usual practices and become aware of how they generally come up with ideas. They then must distinguish their present learning habits from what the rules require of them. In other words, they must practice metacognition—that is, think about their thinking and about how they are being invited to ask questions. They become newly and keenly aware of a structured process. Students also are provided with a disciplined framework within which they are being challenged—directly—to not stop the flow of their thinking and to think in questions. This is a divergent thinking challenge and opportunity.

Producing questions is the next step in the process. The teacher presents the QFocus to the students and gives them a set amount of time to follow the Rules for Producing Questions and come up with their own questions. Students are invited to ask all kinds of questions—an exercise in divergent thinking. The teacher may need to guide students when they show any tendency to violate one or more of the rules.

The next step is to work on improving the questions. *Closed- and open-ended questions* are defined and discussed once the students have finished generating their questions. The teacher introduces a definition of closed- and open-ended questions, which the students use to categorize the list of questions they have just produced. Then the teacher leads the class through a discussion of the advantages and disadvantages of both kinds of questions. To conclude this step, the teacher asks the students to change at least one open-ended question into a closed-ended one and vice versa.

The process of analyzing the advantages and disadvantages of each kind of question encourages another level of metacognition as students think about the role and purpose of questions, the particular structure of a question, and how manipulating its wording can block or yield certain information. This discovery of the nature of questions allows them to think about the inquiry process in a new way. Then, as they work on changing the form of questions from one to the other, they must think about what they will find out, how the formulation meets their needs, and how it can enhance their inquiry process that began with a purely divergent exercise. They begin to think convergently.

Once they have explored the nature of closed- and open-ended questions, students begin to *prioritize* them. Prioritization of questions may be based on a variety of criteria. The teacher, with the lesson plan in mind, offers guidelines and asks the students to look at their questions and come to an agreement about which are their priority questions. Usually, but not always, the teachers asks for three selections.

The students begin to look at the relative merits of the questions they have selected and how these questions will help them get the information they need. They must compare the questions to each other and assess which will be most helpful. They also begin to look at sequential matters, pondering which question would have to be answered first before the others could be answered or even considered. They are thinking again about the nature of a question, the information it will yield, and how to most effectively use the questions they themselves generated.

After this metacognition process, students are in a better position to think convergently, select their priority questions, and move on to *next steps* informed by the prioritization process. Teacher and students discuss a plan for how to use the questions developed in the previous steps. The teacher may give instructions on what is now to be done with the priority questions.

Reflection, the final step involves both content and process. The teacher will now ask the students a few questions, shifting back to familiar territory in which the teacher asks and the students respond. The questions can cover different areas of the process, asking students to think about and name what they learned, how they learned it, what is different about what they know or understand or want to know now than at the beginning, and how can they use what they learned, both in terms of content and skills.

In this step, the students are engaged in thinking about their thinking and learning process. They are naming not only what they learned but also how they learned it. This metacognition reinforces learning related both to content and skills. Because they are being asked to put their experience into words, they are able to think broadly about it. Because there will be different lessons for different students, as they hear from others in the class, students begin to think divergently about all that can be learned from the process. Finally, as they conclude and name what was most important for them individually, they are thinking convergently, bringing their ideas together into conclusions.

THE ART AND SCIENCE OF THE QUESTION FORMULATION TECHNIQUE

The use of the QFT in the classroom is both an art and a science. It is an art because you are drawing on your implicit knowledge and the finely honed skills that allow you to creatively facilitate a range of individual, small group, and whole class learning experiences. It is a science because you are using a protocol—a series of tested, proven procedures that consistently produce this result: students think in new and deeper ways and can name those changes themselves.

Here is how art and science manifest in the Question Formulation Technique:

The Art

Design of the QFocus: This requires some creativity and imagination as well as a willingness to test and explore what works; it is meant to foster continuous improvement—much like the use of a traditional prompt.

Student group work: This is always an art and hardly ever a science. The dynamics of interactions and group composition can affect student work. Since these interactions shift and vary from group to group and moment to moment, managing group processes is always more of an art than a science.

Producing questions and changing of closed- and open-ended questions: This is a process the students get better at the more they practice.

Prioritization: Teacher instructions and student interests, knowledge, preferences, and dynamics all affect the emergence of priority questions; this process of growth and change requires creativity. As students get more practice prioritizing and justifying their choice of priority questions, they become better at these activities.

Next steps: Teachers or students or teachers and students together construct and shape the success of how questions will be used, a process that varies with every set of questions and assignments.

The Science

Adherence to one cardinal laboratory rule: Students ask their own questions; they do not respond to a teacher's question. This produces replicable results in the classroom cum laboratory where students are using a rigorous protocol for producing, improving, and prioritizing their own questions.

Use of the QFocus: Simply by presenting a focus for student questions, the dynamics of the classroom are changed. Students are now asking questions. They may produce only a few questions, but this is measurably more than they would have produced without the change to using a QFocus.

The Rules for Producing Questions: These are the minimum number of rules needed in order to get students to do something different—to start producing their own questions. Each works in conjunction with the others and together, they effectively provide both a creative and disciplined structure within which students can produce their own questions.

Knowledge of the nature of closed- and open-ended questions: This is often new knowledge for students, and it can be transformative as they see how the manipulation of a question allows them to get different information.

Reflection: This seems like such an open-ended invitation to thinking that it belongs more on the art side of the ledger. But regular use can produce consistent, replicable results by providing students with an unusual opportunity to name for themselves what they learned, how they learned it, and how they plan to use it.

In the chapters that follow, the full art and science of the Question Formulation Technique will come to life in the work of teachers and students.

The RQI Question Formulation Technique™

- **Produce** Your Own Questions
- **Improve** Your Questions
- **Prioritize** Your Questions

Produce Your Questions

Four essential rules for producing your own questions:

- Ask as many questions as you can.
- Do not stop to discuss, judge or answer the questions.
- Write down every question *exactly* as it is stated.
- Change any statement into a question.

Improve Your Questions

Categorize the questions as closed- or open-ended:

- **Closed-ended questions:** They can be answered with yes or no or with one word.
- **Open-ended questions:** They require an explanation and cannot be answered with yes or no or with one word.

Find closed-ended questions. Mark them with a *c*.

The other questions must be open-ended. Mark them with an *o*.

Name the value of each type of question:

- The advantages and disadvantages of asking closed-ended questions.
- The advantages and disadvantages of asking open-ended questions

Change questions from one type to another:

- Change closed-ended questions to open-ended.
- Change open-ended questions to closed-ended.

Prioritize the Questions

Choose your three most important questions:

1.

2.

3.

Why did you choose these three as the most important?

Next Steps

How are you going to you use your questions?

CHAPTER 2

Choose the Question Focus

The Starting Point for Student Questions

"I learned that asking questions is such a simple thing but, at the same time, can open up towards so much opportunity to learn."

A YOUNG HIGH SCHOOL SCIENCE TEACHER in Los Angeles, in the second year of her Teach for America placement, wrote to us that having learned how to better manage the class, her goal for the new year was to get students thinking for themselves. She had asked herself, "How can I push my students to apply their critical thinking skills?" And she had her own answer: by asking a question and further engaging them in their exploration of the topic. "Unfortunately, I have not developed this skill," she wrote, "This is the area in which I am asking for your guidance."

TEACHER'S QUESTION AS THE PROMPT: A VENERABLE TRADITION

This young teacher had placed herself squarely in a venerable tradition of teachers dedicated to finding the perfect question that will stimulate student thinking. The *prompt* is part of the essential vocabulary and core tools that the teacher brings each day to the classroom. And nothing is more central to the traditional prompting of student thinking than the teacher's question. It is, indeed, the standard by which wise teaching has been measured for the twenty-five hundred years since Socrates got into trouble asking questions that forced his students to examine their unexamined lives. Socrates created a model that has been sustained for millennia, maintaining the instructor's tight control over the questioning process. Socrates, as teacher, got to ask the questions. The students were to reply to his line of questioning, wherever it went.

And so has it been ever since. Teachers are trained from the very beginnings of their career to design prompts to stimulate student thinking. Every teacher who has ever planned a classroom discussion, from kindergarten through higher education, has spent time preparing, reviewing, evaluating a range of options for prompting students to start talking and thinking (the two don't always come together) about the day's key lesson or theme. Desperately seeking ways to ignite the fire of enthusiasm and curiosity in their students, teachers regularly add to their already onerous workload trying to figure out prompts that will unleash student creativity and problem-solving ability. Some teachers have told us how they spent an entire summer ruminating about what might be the perfect "essential question" that would guide a year's worth of study and provoke new student thinking. If not a whole summer, there are certainly many weekends and evenings devoted, as a middle school teacher in Atlanta told us, to coming up with the exact questions that would start students thinking for themselves as they began a major research project. "Something is wrong with this picture," she concluded, realizing that the students, not the teacher, need the opportunity to work hard on coming up with their own questions.

FROM THE TRADITIONAL PROMPT TO A NEW QUESTION FOCUS

When you use the Question Formulation Technique, you are making one significant change in the traditional dynamic in the classroom: from using your question to prompt student thinking and work to challenging students to come up with their own questions. The key change in practice starts with a change in name. Out goes the term prompt, and in its place, we use Question Focus, or QFocus. The name is meant as a reminder: to you, that your role is to provide a focus for student questions; and to students, as a notice that your QFocus is not a question for them to answer but, rather, a focus, for questions that they will create.

> **Question Focus:** *A stimulus for jumpstarting student questions. It can be a short statement or a visual or aural aid in any medium or format that can stimulate student thinking that will be expressed through their questions. It is the opposite of using a teacher's question to prompt student thinking.*

You may be using the QFocus to help students get unstuck by using the QFT on the spot, or you may be using it as part of a fully developed plan for a lesson, unit, or an entire curriculum. Yet even if you are using a QFocus and deploying the QFT for the first time—and discovering the shift in practice that comes with that—you are also playing a very familiar role. You remain in charge; you are still guiding the instructional process with your goals and objectives in mind. You are deciding when, where, and for what purpose you require students to develop their own questions.

WHAT MAKES AN EFFECTIVE QUESTION FOCUS?

As you probably know from experience, designing effective prompts is an ongoing learning process. You get better at it the more you do it and the more you see how the phrasing and timing of prompts affect student responses—how which ones work better for which students and which points in the curriculum. Your facility in using prompts reflects your deep implicit knowledge of what will work.

You will develop a similar level of implicit knowledge, which you will also be able to make explicit to yourself and to colleagues, the more you practice designing and using a QFocus to stimulate students' questions. Teachers who have had relatively little experience designing a QFocus quickly learn how to create and fine-tune one that will meet the needs of the students and the lessons to be taught. Their experiences point to a few basic criteria to keep in mind for creating an effective QFocus:

1. **It has a clear focus:** Keep in mind the importance of the word *focus*. The issue, topic, area of concern, and main emphasis should be brief and simply stated. Students will generate questions more easily when the QFocus is sharply delineated.
2. **It is *not* a question:** The purpose is to get the students to start asking *their own* questions.

These two guidelines alone will allow you to design an effective QFocus. Some teachers have also found that two more guidelines are helpful:

1. **It provokes and stimulates new lines of thinking:** A provocative QFocus can stimulate a strong response and a flurry of questions

2. **It does not reveal teacher preferences or bias:** It is better if the QFocus is not a restatement of what students will recognize as the teacher's opinion. The QFocus should give students opportunity to think freely.

These points may be obvious to you, especially since points 1, 3, and 4 are also elements of effective traditional prompts. As you recognize this, you know that this is really all about point 2: students are asking the questions, not you. But it also means that points 1, 3, and 4 must be considered in the context of this critical guideline. In the next section, you can read more about each guideline as it is reflected in teachers' classroom experiences. After that, we will lead you through a process in which you will design your own QFocus (a worksheet for this process is provided in this chapter's appendix).

It Has a Clear Focus

If the focus is not clear, the students will spend too much intellectual energy trying to understand it. Too many small details or references to other points, and the students are likely to become distracted. The QFocus is more effective when it is:

- **Brief and simply stated:** Teachers have successfully used a QFocus that consists of a short statement or simple phrase or topic:
  - Evolution of the eye
  - The structure of fractions
  - Your rights are protected by the Constitution
- **Sharply focused:** You want to draw the students' attention in a certain direction. You also want to engage and stimulate them enough to ask questions towards a specific area or creating a sense of urgency. Sometimes if the QFocus is too broad or vague students will have difficulty formulating questions.

The following examples demonstrate how some teachers developed a clear QFocus. Lisa Onsum, a biology teacher at Boston Day and Evening Academy (BDEA), teaches an entry-level science class. The class was starting a unit on cellular biology, and she knew some students were already familiar with the subject and just needed a review while others needed a full introduction. She considered this QFocus:

The cell

However, she realized that this formulation was too broad and would not offer students a sharp-enough hook to start their questioning process. After considering other options, she decided to use this one:

The inside of a cell

It was more granular and allowed students with different levels of knowledge to ask specific questions from their own perspective.

Charlese Harris, who teaches math at BDEA, regularly encountered students who were convinced they simply could not do math and were fearful of studying it. She considered using a very simple QFocus to get them to think in different ways about their fear:

Math anxiety

But as she tried to play out what questions they might ask, she realized that her wording was too general. She changed it to:

Defeating math anxiety

The addition of the word *defeating* allowed students to start thinking proactively about what they could actually do to overcome their fear. Harris's modification of the QFocus highlights how inserting an active word (verb or gerund) can make a QFocus far more effective.

Yana Minchenko, a humanities teacher at BDEA, had a similar experience. She used a one-word QFocus to go along with the reading of a short story that examined a teenager's life choices and the impact they had:

Choices

Minchenko found that it was hard for students to ask questions about this QFocus; they responded as they would when she'd ask, "Are there any questions?" There might be a few questions, but they didn't flow easily. So she amended the QFocus to:

The choices we make

With the new wording, Minchenko saw immediate and palpable changes: students leaned forward instead of back; they looked carefully at the questions as they were being recorded; and generated a number of questions that had not been elicited by the previous QFocus.

It Is *Not* a Question

You may be accustomed to prompting students with questions. But because students are definitely accustomed to responding to questions rather than generating their own, it would be very confusing if you were to use your own question as a QFocus.

This does not mean you will *never* use a question to stimulate more questions. A question can work effectively, but your students may need to gain more experience and confidence in asking their own questions before you use a QFocus in question format.

It Provokes and Stimulates New Lines of Thinking

You can create a QFocus to challenge student assumptions and push your students to see the topic or task at hand from different perspectives. The *provocative* element will help them produce questions more quickly. Marcy Ostberg, for example, transformed a mild-mannered QFocus in her biology class at BDEA into a provocative one by inserting one key word. Her students generally do not like hearing that they *must* do something. They managed to probe further and gain a much deeper understanding of the scientific method when she asked them to generate questions in response to:

The scientific method must *be followed*

Another high school history teacher, Ariela Rothstein, while teaching a unit on immigrants and civil rights, used the case of *Miranda v. Arizona* to develop this QFocus:

Miranda Rights always *protects the rights of the accused*

The word *always* in this QFocus raises questions immediately. Consider how your thinking changes if you remove the word. The statement can still function as an effective QFocus, but it will not necessarily light a fire for quickly producing a lot of questions.

It Does Not Reveal Teacher Preferences or Bias

Since the goal of the QFocus is to give students freedom to think, be careful about letting students know your preferences or giving too much direction. You have seen many times how students spend time trying to figure out the answer they think you want instead of doing their own thinking. You have to pay attention to the way you phrase the QFocus for the same reason—your students may spend too much intellectual energy on coming up with the questions they think you'd want them to ask.

If, for example, you have taught a full unit in which you have been waxing poetic about how Emerson, Thoreau, and the Transcendentalists were the most profound thinkers in American history and you were trying to be provocative, you might use as a QFocus:

Transcendentalism was an unimportant philosophical movement

Even though this might not be your opinion, your students would be on to you, and the QFocus would be more likely to produce confusion than to stimulate new divergent thinking. You could instead create safe space for them to question what they already know as your position by using:

The importance of transcendentalism in American history

By asking questions about this QFocus, which may include looking at historical impact, criteria, standards, perspectives, interests, biases, relevance, etc., students are given license not only to explore but also to question what they know to be your position. Alternatively, you could switch the focus from the particular and have them work on the more general:

Criteria for assessing the importance of a philosopher

Coming at the end of the unit, this version allows students to take what they have learned and generalize their thinking. Giving them the opportunity to ask questions rather than respond to a prompt (e.g., "What are possible criteria for assessing the importance of a philosopher?") opens up the possibility for new ways of thinking, including ways that may be different than yours.

This fourth guideline can be challenging to follow. If the QFocus reflects your preferences, you may inadvertently be guiding the direction of the questions—and you may be tempted to do so. You are, after all, setting a learning agenda by designing the QFocus. You know where the curriculum leads and what upcoming tests will require of students. It can feel like it is an abdication of teacher responsibility to refrain from guiding student thinking in a certain direction. But crossing the fine line from pedagogical direction to personal bias will limit student independent thinking.

In the rest of the chapter, we will take you through all the steps from defining purpose to evaluating the QFocus and show examples of how other teachers have handled this challenge.

DESIGNING A QFOCUS

The process for creating the QFocus is as familiar as creating an effective prompt, but the shift to a QFocus from a prompt approach initially requires some practice. Although you can try a variety of ideas, designing any QFocus comprises five basic steps (see table 2.1). It starts with a clarification of your purpose.

Why Do You Want Students to Formulate Questions?

The selection or design of a Question Focus has to start with the end in sight. What is the purpose of having students ask their own questions? How are students going to use the questions they generate?

You can use this technique once or several times in the same unit with different goals in mind: to generate interest at the beginning of a unit, introduce a topic, assess where students are or deepen comprehension in the middle of the unit, stimulate new lines of inquiry, prepare for a long-term assignment, or conclude a unit with questions for further study. Designing the QFocus requires that you think about what students will be doing *after they work on their questions*: will they be doing a research project, writing an essay, conducting an experiment, or using the questions as a guide for reading or are you just having students generate questions to stimulate their thinking or for you to use in planning the class?

Once your purpose is clear, you can move on to the other four steps—generating possible QFocus ideas, identifying the pros and cons for each idea, choosing the QFocus you will use and assessing it against the criteria for a good QFocus, and finally imagining the kinds of questions you expect the QFocus to provoke. The

TABLE 2.1

Steps for designing a QFocus

1. Define the purpose	What do you want to accomplish by using the QFocus? Keep your teaching goals and learning outcomes in mind.
	• Generate interest.
	• Stimulate new thinking.
	• Deepen comprehension.
	• Gather information about student understanding.
2. Generate possible ideas	List several ideas for possible QFocus. Keep in mind your purpose and what students will be doing with the questions. List all kinds of ideas in different formats: statements, pictures, etc. Listing a variety of ideas is key for finding and effective focus. Sometimes first idea that comes to mind is not the best to achieve your purpose. Having several ideas will allow you to evaluate and choose one that best meets the criteria and fits your purpose.
	Think about several ways to present the same idea.
	• List statements, visual and other strategies.
	• Look for simple ideas.
	• Keep statements as brief and simple as possible.
3. Identify pros and cons for each idea	Look at each QFocus idea you have listed and think about what will be the pros and cons. Keep in mind the criteria when identifying pros and cons:
	• Has a clear focus
	• Is *not* a question
	• Provokes and stimulates new lines of thinking
	• Does not show teacher preference or bias
	This part of the process will allow you to do an initial assessment and narrow down the ideas that will help you meet your purpose.
4. Choose one QFocus idea and assess against four criteria	Choose one of the ideas from your list that best meets your purpose and see if meets the four criteria listed in step 3. If the QFocus doesn't meet the criteria you can rephrase it or choose and assesses another idea. You can easily rephrase it by adding or deleting words. If it meets the criteria, go to the next step of design.
5. Imagine questions students may come up with	You now have a QFocus that can fit your purpose. As a last step think about possible questions your students might ask. The purpose of this step is to try to assess the potential of the focus in helping students produce questions and the direction the questions might go. You will not be using these questions.

following two case studies provide a glimpse into the thinking of two teachers as they designed a QFocus.

DESIGNING A QFOCUS IN AN URBAN HIGH SCHOOL HUMANITIES CLASS

Consider the development of this QFocus by Ling-Se Peet, a high school humanities teacher in Boston. Her class was reading the novel *In the Time of the Butterflies* by Julia Alvarez, in which torture is used by the brutal Trujillo regime in the Dominican Republic. She wanted the students to grapple with the purposes and practices of torture as they read the book and make connections with current events around this issue.

She found data about American attitudes about the use of torture against suspected terrorists and crafted this QFocus:

> *There is a recent poll by the Pew Research Center that found that 71 percent of Americans—American adults—said torture can be justified often or sometimes or rarely. Only 25 percent said never.*[1]

Would this be an effective QFocus? It depends on the purpose of using the QFT. If Peet were teaching a class on polling techniques or changing American attitudes on key issues, she might want the students to consider the difficulties in pinning down specific attitudes. She also might want them to explore how the poll was constructed or implemented and what kinds of conclusions can be drawn. If these were her goals or the content she would be teaching, then the survey data might serve her purposes well because the QFocus could stimulate thinking about these different directions.

A QFocus, however, can suffer from too much information. The students could get stuck on different percentages, the name of a specific polling source, and gradations of acceptance, all of which would distract them from focusing on torture's moral and political meaning.

Peet chose to use this QFocus instead:

> *Torture can be justified*

This wording would serve her purpose well. Student could zero in on major themes related to the purposes of torture and generate questions about punishment versus torture and justifiable actions versus inhumane ones. You will get to read about the questions the students produced in chapters 4 and 6.

DESIGNING A QFOCUS IN AN URBAN HIGH SCHOOL SCIENCE CLASS

Marcy Ostberg was doing a unit on pollution. She wanted students to understand why it was important to study this topic, engage them in the topic, deepen comprehension, and also develop a research project. She found a quotation from a speech Al Gore gave that she thought could help them understand why their study of pollution was so important:[2]

> There are many who still do not believe that global warming is a problem at all. And it's no wonder: because they are the targets of a massive and well-organized campaign of disinformation lavishly funded by polluters who are determined to prevent any action to reduce the greenhouse gas emissions that cause global warming out of a fear that their profits might be affected if they had to stop dumping so much pollution into the atmosphere.

Ostberg prepared to build her lesson around the quotation. Then she looked at it again to see if it presented a compelling case for her students to learn more.

It could work for certain purposes: if Ostberg wanted the students to study the politics behind Gore's statement; if she wanted them to learn more about Gore's position on environmental issues or his role in warning the world about global warming; or if she wanted them to examine more closely disinformation as related to global warming. She stopped to assess her choice of a QFocus and thought about pros and cons (see table 2.2). The quotation was definitely not a simple one. It could easily take the students off on many paths, following the trail of some of the details that were not directly relevant to the work ahead of them. And the reference to Al Gore could draw a good bit of attention to the man who was being quoted instead of the science behind the statement. The last thing Ostberg wanted to do was to distract students from the focused work she had planned for them. She needed them to begin to think about and identify topics for research papers or experiments. Gore's political analysis was going to be too broad for her students. She needed to help them focus more sharply.

Ostberg's experience demonstrates how the teacher as designer of the QFocus is not relinquishing authority or responsibility to set learning objectives, tie a lesson

TABLE 2.2

Assessing a proposed QFocus

Pros	Cons
• Students could learn about Gore's opinion	• Not simple
• Not a question	• Not sharply focused
	• Details not directly relevant to work ahead
	• Person quoted could draw too much attention
	• Could distract from asking questions about science behind statement

plan to the overall curriculum, or encourage student interest in a specific topic. Even as she is temporarily giving the power of asking questions to the students, she maintains her instructional leadership role in the design of the QFocus.

Ostberg decided that instead of the Gore quote, to come up with a new list of possible QFocus ideas:

1. Pollution.
2. Pollution harms Boston residents.
3. Earth Day has fixed all pollution problems.
4. If pollution is harmful, prove it.
5. Pollution is destroying the earth.
6. 2–3 images of pollution

She then named the pros and cons of each focus idea (see table 2.3).

After considering the pros and cons of each one she decided to use "Pollution harms Boston residents" as the focus and assessed that QFocus against the four criteria discussed above (see table 2.4). This focus clearly met two of the criteria and also gave a sense of immediacy to the issue.

In the final step of the design process, Ostberg thought about possible questions students would ask: what kind of pollution harms residents, how it harms them, where is the most pollution in Boston, how can pollution be addressed? etc.

Ostberg decided to take her Qfocus a step further by looking at specific types of pollution—from traffic, factories, and eutrophication. Her students could use the

TABLE 2.3

Naming Pros and Cons for QFocus Ideas

QFocus ideas	Pros	Cons
1. Pollution.	Short and sweet; they have a lot of background info to build on.	Too broad; lacks focus.
2. Pollution harms Boston residents.	Pushes them to thinking more about our local community.	May be narrow.
3. Earth Day has fixed all pollution problems.	Looked at Earth Day pictures yesterday that showed otherwise.	Too broad.
4. If pollution is harmful, prove it.	Experiment-specific questions, helping them think about what can be tested and why.	Too quickly gives them a task; the QFocus of *pollution is harmful* or *pollution is not harmful* would work better.
5. Pollution is destroying the earth.	Possible research focus; reminds them about some of the things we have been talking about.	Does not narrow the ideas; also makes them think outside of our community.
6. 2–3 images of pollution.	Different teaching media.	Too many options; how to know which images are appropriate?

same focus to explore all these areas. In chapters 4 and 6 you can see the questions the students produced.

TROUBLESHOOTING DESIGNING A QFOCUS

Just like the process for generating an effective prompt, the more you practice, the easier it will become to develop an effective Qfocus. Here are some recommendations:

- Try to choose a single purpose and keep the QFocus as simple as possible. Because the technique is flexible, you will be able to use the process with different QFocus statements multiple times in any unit.
- Make sure to generate as many ideas as possible or brainstorm your QFocus ideas. Do not skip the step of assessing your ideas against the criteria.

TABLE 2.4

Assessing a QFocus against four criteria

Proposed QFocus: *Pollution harms Boston residents*

	Does Q-Focus meet criteria?		
Criteria for assessing QFocus	*Yes*	*No*	*Maybe*
Has a clear focus	X		
Is *not* a question	X		
Provokes and stimulates new lines of thinking			X
Does not reveal teacher preferences or biases			X

- Imagine what questions you might ask. Test out colleagues about what they might ask in response to your QFocus. Test out two or three examples.
- Have a backup plan. Plan alternative ways of presenting your QFocus ahead of time. This will help you problem solve if you find that the QFocus you originally chose fails in helping students produce questions.
- Keeping your own preferences or biases out of the QFocus could be the most difficult part of the four criteria to follow. Keep it in mind, but do not get overly concerned about it. Instead, after using the QFocus, think about if you gave too much or too little direction and adjust next time you use the QFT process.
- When using pictures, diagrams, or equations as a QFocus, you also need to think about how to frame them clearly. Along with any visuals or specific items used as part of your QFocus, you still need a statement framing what you are presenting. Otherwise, the students will not know what they are expected to focus on and will not generate questions. The accompanying statement must meet the criteria for an effective QFocus.

CONCLUSION

Now you have to get your students ready to start asking questions. But, first, they need some time to consider the significance of the rules for producing questions and what will be required of them when they start coming up with their own questions.

Key Points

- The design of an effective QFocus is very similar to the work you do in designing an effective prompt.
- The QFocus should be designed to stimulate student questions.
- The design of the QFocus will depend on your purpose, as well as when and where in a unit or lesson you are using the QFT.
- Generate as many QFocus ideas as possible as part of process for developing an effective focus.

CHAPTER 3

Introduce the Rules for Producing Questions

An Exercise in Metacognition

*"When you ask your own questions
you're basically challenging yourself."*

A T THIS POINT, you have already given much thought to why you are using the QFT and how it fits into your lesson plan. You have designed a Question Focus that will serve to start the students' questioning process. Where do you begin with it? What is required to create a rigorously structured process that opens the door to new ideas and broader thinking—those desirable, often elusive, outcomes of productive divergent thinking? Through a long process of trial and error, we have distilled the best practices for divergent thinking into four rules. Once the QFocus is ready, your next step is to introduce your students to what we call the *Rules for Producing Questions*:

1. Ask as many questions as you can.
2. Do not stop to discuss, judge, or answer any question.
3. Write down every question exactly as it is stated.
4. Change any statement into a question.

These are potent tools for getting students to begin asking questions. They are deceptively simple; your students might quickly glance at them, dismiss them as not particularly significant, shrug, and wait for further instructions. But looks can be deceiving. The rules were a long time in the making—getting them down to just four took seven years. During those seven long years we tried out and tossed aside a few dozen guidelines that could be invoked to push and prod a divergent thinking process. Our goal was to make something "as simple as possible, and no further" as Einstein said. Of course, Carl Jung had his own take on that: "It would be a simple enough thing to do if only simplicity were not the most difficult of all things."[1] Perhaps, the best description of what we tried to do with creating only four rules is to follow the dictum of the modern composer Earl Kim (mentor to the cellist Yo Yo Ma), who said the goal is "to reduce everything to its maximum."[2] Eventually, we found that these were the specific formulations that could consistently produce the same or even better results than burdening instructors and learners with too many rules.

Each of the four rules facilitates a behavior that contributes to effective question formulation (see table 3.1). When they are used together, the results are striking. Teachers see dramatic improvement in engagement and depth of thinking. Ever in search of making things as simple as possible, we have occasionally tried dropping one or another of the rules, but quickly see that it can't be done. Taking away any one of the four undermines the Question Formulation Technique; the magic disappears and the thinking process gets gummed up.

TABLE 3.1

Changes that result from use of the Rules for Producing Questions

Rule	*What does it accomplish?*
1. Ask as many questions as you can.	Gives license to ask
2. Do not stop to discuss, judge, or answer any question.	Creates safe space and protection
3. Write down every question exactly as it is stated.	Levels the playing field so all questions and voices are respected
4. Change any statement into a question.	Insists on the discipline of phrasing, asking, and thinking in questions, not statements

DISCOVERING THE CHALLENGES AND VALUE OF DISCUSSING THE RULES FOR PRODUCING QUESTIONS

Can *rules* and *divergent thinking* play nicely together? They seem like such polar opposites—one demanding constraint and setting limits, the other encouraging speculation, conjecture, and open-ended exploration headed in multiple directions.

But when you ask students to take on a new intellectual task, one that could tax them and stretch them in utterly new ways, they will need a structure to guide them in the process. The Rules for Producing Questions give shape and structure to an open-ended thinking process and reduce students' anxiety when they undertake what can be one of the most unnerving of all experiences: a reversal of roles—from responding to your questions to having to come up with their own.

The Rules for Producing Questions are carefully scaffolded on each other; each one makes the next a stronger resource to help students learn to produce their own questions. We will look at each rule in turn to see the role it plays in allowing the students to do divergent thinking.

Rule 1: Ask as Many Questions as You Can

This rule seems clear enough. Go ahead. Ask questions. What could sound simpler?

But wisdom and painful experiences have already taught many of us that it's not that simple. Put us in front of a car mechanic, a lawyer, someone with a white coat and a stethoscope and, all of sudden, nothing could seem more difficult. Generating questions in settings beyond one's domain and expertise is a difficult intellectual task. It is an ability honed and tested by years of professional training and experience. The expert in any setting is not just the one who possesses more knowledge—the one capable of giving answers—but also the one who knows *what to ask*.

That's why this first rule, if presented on its own, can leave some students with blank looks on their faces. And a blank stare may be the nicest look you'll see; it is easier to handle than an overwhelmed, confused, frustrated, and annoyed one saying: "What d'you mean, asking me to come up with questions?! That's *your* job!"

Those students may be right. It *has* been the teacher's job for as long as they've experienced formal education. And you know as well that it's been the teacher's job as long as you've been teaching.

Thus the rule "Ask as many questions as you can" may not be sufficient to get all students started. So what does it accomplish all by itself, without regard to or backup from the other rules?

For some students—although probably not the majority—it can be a game changer. In classroom after classroom, you can see the wheels starting to turn as these students get past the initial few moments of silence and resistance. They get a look that says, "This is exciting!" as if they wondered why they've never had this opportunity before. There's pent-up intellectual energy that has been waiting to be released. This rule gives them *license to ask*.

Rule 2: Do Not Stop to Discuss, Judge, or Answer Any Question

The first rule is necessary for getting the question formulation process started but, as we noted above, not necessarily sufficient to get the majority of your students asking questions. It needs help. That's where the second rule comes in.

Rule 1 gives students the license to ask questions; rule 2 takes away the right to discuss the questions, for the moment. The first rule is a positive commandment; the second is a negative injunction with three separate parts.

Do Not Stop to Discuss: An Efficiency Tool. The second rule demands unnatural behavior. A question is raised and yet no one is allowed to respond, discuss, or share any of the thoughts it may have provoked. The process requires that a question—any question—can be followed only by another question. Each time a question is asked, the same rule applies; keep asking more questions but don't stop to discuss them.

Why? Stopping the flow of questions that rule 1 promotes would not allow for the "having lots of questions" process. The rule is rooted in far too many experiences in which the first question raised in a discussion or meeting gets exhaustively discussed for a full hour. Only then, when everyone is worn out by the debate, does someone suggest that maybe the focus has been on the "wrong" question.

Although spending time on questions rather than going right to answers can seem like a detour, it can wind up being a shortcut,because no time is wasted on discussing questions that may not be productive for your students. But neither your students nor you can quite know what's worth discussing until they have a chance (and you enforce the rule) to produce and see many questions before going on with the next steps of the QFT.

Do Not Judge: An Equalizing Force. There's more than efficiency at play in rule 2. It brings a subtle but powerful countervailing force to students' traditional experiences of being silenced or steered.

The "do not judge" component of this rule emerged as we observed the challenges faced by people who not only rarely ask questions, but whose voices are also rarely respected when they do speak up. Asking a question can be an act of courage, and nothing will as quickly prevent that person from ever taking the risk a second time as hearing a snap judgment that may burst out as "That's a stupid question" or—more subtly, genuinely, or manipulatively—"Hmm, I think it's better to think about it this way, or to ask this other question . . ."

Either way, shutdown occurs. And it happens all the time. Be it in the classroom, in the faculty room or in corporate business meetings, questions are tentatively asked and then judgments are made and conversations are stopped. It happens in classrooms where students with perfect SAT scores might be fearful of sounding stupid, and it happens as well in classrooms where students are grades behind their peers in reading levels and have absorbed a message that sadly makes them believe they *are* stupid. Rule 2 is designed to change that dynamic—and even eliminate the prefatory statements made by hesitant students who have internalized another fear of judgment: "This may sound stupid, but . . . ," or "I know this is a stupid question, but . . ."

Invoking and following this rule can go a long way to changing the unintended, but noticeable undercurrent that too often neutralizes independent thinking.

Do Not Answer: An Opening, Not a Closing, to Ideas. A nasty comment from a classmate is intimidating enough. But, there may actually be one thing that will stop a divergent thinking process even more quickly than a snap judgment: an answer.

Just as stopping to discuss one question will block the asking of more questions, so will the attempt to answer a question, even when it seems that there is an obvious answer—a small factual matter. And, of course, what seems like an obvious answer to some may not appear that way to others, and a "simple, quick" answer can undermine the entire process. There will be a place and time in the process for students to work on answers to questions, but this is the stage for divergent thinking—and answers must yield here to questions—*only* questions.

These three negative injunctions—do not stop to discuss, do not judge, and do not answer—are specific mechanisms that, more than anything else, *create room for and safe space for the question formulation process to take hold.*

Rule 3: Write Down Every Question Exactly as It Is Stated

For generations, teachers have been trained to help their students by rephrasing student questions, adding a word here, dropping one there, changing a word, or, if deemed necessary, even the meaning of the question, to make the question fit better for teaching and learning purposes. Sometimes consciously, sometimes by habit, teachers wind up doing the thinking for their students.

Rebecca Steinitz, a coach for WriteBoston, an organization that helps teachers foster writing skills across all disciplines, was dumbstruck by the significance of this rule. "I've taught at all levels, including at the college level, and I can now hear myself and see myself when I was changing my students' questions all the time: 'Oh, so you're really asking . . .' or 'So, you mean to ask . . .' or I just take it and without a word of explanation change a word or two or three and put the 'much improved' question on the board." But, as she recalled doing it, she realized "I wasn't necessarily 'improving' their question, I was shaping it to what I thought should be asked. And we as teachers are explicitly encouraged to do that, to take a student's question and mold it to what we want all the class to be thinking about."[3]

Changing the question, as Steinitz names it clearly, is a time-honored, innocently executed, well-intentioned act, reinforced by a long tradition of teaching practice. Rule 3 changes all that. It honors and validates the question—building, rather than undermining, the confidence of the student who contributed it. It also gives the students full ownership of the questions being produced and allows for all voices to be heard. *Essentially, it levels the playing field so all questions and voices are respected.*

Once students know about this rule they can help each other, and hold the recorder and themselves accountable about writing the questions exactly as stated.

Rule 4: Change Any Statement into a Question

"This is a strange rule," one teacher at the Boston Day and Evening Academy observed when she first encountered it: "The whole point here is to ask questions. Why would you even need this rule?"

It does indeed seem strange, except that many people think they are asking a question when they are really making a statement. The sloppy use of the term and form of a question makes it harder to separate some expressions of intent from those of inquiry. We have seen in session after session, among highly educated groups and those with limited literacy, how statements are made and those who uttered them are convinced they just asked a question. Students often think they are asking a question because they want to know something about what they uttered. But they have great difficulty putting their concerns into question format.

Can the habit be tamed? Not easily, but this rule helps. Let's look at the difference between these between questionlike statements and real questions:

"Nobody can explain why that happened."

This is tricky because it actually has the *why* word embedded in it, but the expression is an assertion, not a question, and maybe an inaccurate one. The students need the discipline of this rule so they can take that statement apart and create questions out of it. Given the chance, they will move themselves closer to asking:

"Can someone explain why it happened?"

or

"Why did it happen?"

Sometimes, a rise in intonation at the end of sentence will be considered sufficient to make a sentence a question. A student, for example, may start with "The assignment is hard?" But, when pushed to turn a statement into a question, they could move to: "Is the assignment hard?" And that may lead to: "How hard is the assignment?" The Rules for Producing Questions are not meant to assess the quality of a question, but to insure that questions, and only questions, are asked. Rule 4 insists on *the discipline of phrasing, asking and thinking in questions rather than statements.*

INTRODUCING AND DISCUSSING THE RULES FOR PRODUCING QUESTIONS

You'll need to facilitate a discussion about the value of the Rules for Producing Questions and the challenges in following them before introducing a QFocus (table

3.2 shows teacher and student roles in this discussion). This introduction will help the students internalize a new way of working and thinking as they deliberately produce their own questions. They will also be practicing metacognitive skills as they think about how the rules can help them think in new ways and develop their questions.

When the students are experiencing the QFT for the first time, the process for introducing and discussing the rules takes from five to seven minutes to allow for full reflection and analysis. When you use the QFT process again, the rules can be reviewed more briefly.

Introducing the Rules

Introducing the rules can unfold as follows:

1. **Rules discussion:** Decide how the discussion will take place, for example, using one of the following:
   - Students individually reflect on the rules for two to three minutes. They can then share their thoughts in small groups or report to the large group.
   - Students discuss the rules in small groups for three to four minutes and then report to the large group. One student will serve as recorder. The recorder will also reflect on the rules. Reports to the large group can be done by the reporter or by group members.
   - Students discuss the rules as large group for a minimum of five minutes. You might want to keep a chart of student comments you can use for reviewing and reminding them of the need for the rules.
2. **QFocus:** Let students know that you will be introducing a QFocus that they will be using to generate questions.
3. Introduce the rules:
   - *First use:* Ask students to review the rules and to name challenges in following them. Students discuss the rules in small groups with reports to large group or simply discuss as a large group.
   - *Subsequent use:* Review the rules and remind students of the rules each time the process is used

TABLE 3.2

Teacher and student roles in discussing the rules

Teacher role	*Student role*
• Introduce the rules	• Think about and name challenges in following the rules
• Facilitate a discussion on the challenges of the rules	

Setting New Expectations

Your students may be familiar with traditional brainstorming. It is quite unlikely that they have a lot of experience in focusing solely on producing a large number of questions. So students will need a few minutes to grapple with the implications of the Rules for Producing Questions. It is an important metacognitive exercise, especially the first time students are introduced to the question formulation process. They need time to think about what might be difficult about following individual rules as well as the whole set. They also need to imagine themselves doing the thinking activity and then acting in a different way; stopping some of their habitual responses or ingrained ways of thinking and discussing. It is particularly important to discuss the rules before introducing the QFocus. If students hear the QFocus first, they will start thinking about that and won't be ready to internalize the changes required by the rules.

Discussing the Rules

You will find during the small group discussions or when students share as a large group that there are different opinions about the difficulty of following the rules. Some students might find that one of the rules will be more difficult to follow than another. The difference in opinions should not be a concern; students do not need to agree or reach consensus on this issue. The objective is to build awareness about the rules and their implications for the thinking work ahead. When students do the actual work on producing questions, they will become more aware of challenges of following the rules.

Let's look now at some sample activities for facilitating the discussion. In the first example, students are asked to rate the level of difficulty for following each rule and then provide a rationale for the level of difficulty they chose. In the second example, students look at the rules in general, choose one they find difficult to follow, and provide a rationale.

Example 1: Choosing Level of Difficulty and Rationale. For each rule, name "Will it be easy or difficult to follow this rule *and* why? You can use the following template.

Template for discussing level of difficulty	
1. Ask as many questions as you can.	
__ Easy __ Difficult __ Not sure	Why?
2. Do not stop to answer or discuss the questions.	
__ Easy __ Difficult __ Not sure	Why?
3. Write down every question *exactly* as it is stated.	
__ Easy __ Difficult __ Not sure	Why?
4. Change any statements into questions.	
__ Easy __ Difficult __ Not sure	Why?

The value of this activity is that students will have to think about each one of the rules. Potential responses to this exercise can be:

1. Ask as many questions as you can:
   - Easy—Questions can be asked from the top of your head
   - Easy—This is easy because we talk a lot
2. Do not stop to answer or discuss the questions:
   - Difficult—Because we would want an answer
   - Difficult—We like to discuss
3. Write down every question *exactly* as it is stated:
   - Difficult—It is hard to get everything down as stated
   - Not sure—Sometimes it is hard to write question after question
4. Change any statements into questions:
   - Easy—It is restating
   - Not sure—Might not know what the statement is really asking

Example 2: Naming Difficulties for Following the Rules What do you think can be difficult about following these rules *and* why? Use the following template.

Template for discussing challenges following the rules
What do you think can be difficult about following these rules?
1. Ask as many questions as you can.
2. Do not stop to answer or discuss the questions.
3. Write down every question *exactly* as it is stated.
4. Change any statements into questions.
Explain why:

The value of this activity is that students need to consider the rules in general and name potential difficulties in following them. Typical responses in a discussion about how hard or difficult it may be to follow the rules might be as follows:

1. Ask as many questions as you can:
   - I don't know what to ask.
   - Don't have any questions.
   - It is difficult thinking only about questions.

2. Do not stop to answer or discuss the questions:
   - It might be difficult because if you stop you might debate.
   - When someone asks something, you probably want to answer.

3. Write down every question exactly as it is stated:
   - It can be hard—you hear the question [but] you might miss the words.
   - It might be hard not to edit.

4. Change any statements into questions:
   - It might be hard depending on the statement.
   - It could be hard to write a question with same meaning as statement.

You can choose a range of questions and activities for students to think about and discuss. You should never skip over the discussion of the Rules for Producing Questions when using the QFT for the first or even the second time. The discussion insures that students have the chance to think about the implications of the rules they will use to produce the questions.

TROUBLESHOOTING INTRODUCING AND DISCUSSING THE RULES

Here are some challenges you might find while introducing the rules and some recommendations on how to address them.

You Might Find That Students Find No Difficulties in Following the Rules. Do not worry if students do not think it might be difficult to follow the rules. The process ahead is just an abstract idea at this point. The difficulties will become more apparent when they get into the step of producing questions when they actually have to follow the rules.

If students don't name any potential challenges in following the rules, you can

- Ask, "How are the rules different from the way we usually work?"
- Pick one or more rules and ask, "How can these rules help you produce questions? What do you see that is different in following this rule?"

Students Didn't Cover Key Points About the Difficulties in Following the Rules. There will be opportunities during the process to revisit the rules. Do not tell students about what they missed. The goal is for students to think for themselves. The discussion of the rules sets the stage for how you and students will work together. If you tell them, they will be expecting that you continue doing so and that's exactly the kind of behavior you want to change.

There Is No Consensus Around the Rules. The goal is to think and see the rules from different perspectives and accommodate different opinions. Very often you will not see agreement on whether a rule is easy or difficult to follow. Just validate students with a simple "thank you" for their diverse opinions.

CONCLUSION

Now the students know the rules to follow and how they are expected to work. The next step is to make it very clear that you are now presenting the QFocus and that they, the students, will start producing their own questions.

Key Points: Introducing and Discussing the Rules for Producing Questions

- This should not be a lengthy exercise; five to seven minutes will be enough.
- Students can discuss the rules in small or large groups.
- Do not skip this part of the process.

CHAPTER 4

Students Produce the Questions

Divergent Thinking Unleashed

*"The more you ask questions, the more thoughts come
to your head and it helps expand your learning."*

IT IS TIME FOR YOUR STUDENTS TO PRODUCE THE QUESTIONS. Now, the group work begins in earnest. Ah, group work. Over the years, you have seen how great it can be and how difficult it can be. You have figured out your own methods for troubleshooting and facilitating group processes, and you'll call on some of those skills now. You may think that this time it is going to be even harder because you are about to add a new challenge to the group work process. The students are going to do something they may have never done before: generate their own list of questions.

In this chapter, you'll see students in three very different environments who all started with a blank piece of paper. In a short period of time they covered the blank page into a list of questions that reflected their own thoughts, a new thinking process, and previously unarticulated ideas and concerns all expressed in the form of questions.

THE TEACHER'S ROLE: FACILITATING STUDENTS' PRODUCING THEIR OWN QUESTIONS

In her twelfth-grade humanities class, Ling-Se Peet is using the QFT to help her class of twenty-five students gain a deeper understanding of moral themes in a novel. Marcy Ostberg is using the QFT to help a group of twelve students grapple with an observable phenomenon that is covered in their biology curriculum. Hayley Dupuy is using the QFT in her sixth-grade science class to allow her students to think deeply about their upcoming science project before deciding on a specific topic.

In each of these classrooms, the students manage to produce a range of interesting and insightful questions with just three forms of assistance:

1. The Rules for Producing Questions, which the teachers discuss or review with them before they begin
2. A QFocus that is given to them to start the process
3. Gentle reminders from the teacher during the five- to seven-minute session that they should keep asking questions or that a specific rule is being violated

Students will need a minimum of five minutes for producing questions when they are introduced to the QFT process for the first time. They may need less time as they get more practiced at generating questions, although you may want them to spend more time on this step of the process. The process for producing questions can develop as follows:

1. **Divide class into groups of three to five students:** If the discussion about the rules was held in small groups, students should continue working in the same groups. Each group needs a student to serve as a scribe to write down the questions.
2. **Introduce the QFocus:** Repeat the focus as needed but do not explain it.
3. **Instruct students to produce questions:** Remind them to make sure to follow the rules and to number each question they produce. Let students know how much time they have for producing the questions. About five minutes will be enough for students to produce a list of questions they can use for the next step of the process. Ideally, you will be able step to the side, wander around the room, and listen in as the students are generating their own questions by following the rules.
4. **Monitor students as they work in their small groups:** Check to be sure they are actively working and that they stick to the rules. When you see a problem—for example, if one group is stopping to discuss a question—then your job is to simply bring them back to the task. Do not give examples or questions to students as you support them. Take note of whether students have enough questions in order to complete the upcoming steps in the process and encourage them to ask more if needed.

Table 4.1 summarizes teacher and student roles during the step of producing questions.

TABLE 4-1

Teacher and student roles

Teacher role	Student role
• Introduce the QFocus. • Set the time frame. • Observe group work and remind specific groups or class as a whole to use the Rules for Producing Questions. • Alert students to how much time is left.	• A volunteer or a designated student is selected to record the questions of the group (the scribe should also contribute questions). • Generate questions following the Rules for Producing Questions. • The recorder writes down the questions and numbers them.

CASE STUDY: STUDENTS PRODUCING QUESTIONS IN AN URBAN HIGH SCHOOL

Teacher: Ling-Se Peet, Urban and Sciences Academy (Boston Public Schools)

Subject: Humanities

Class size: Twenty-five students

QFocus: *Torture can be justified*

Purpose in using QFT: Class is reading *In the Time of the Butterflies* by Julia Alvarez, a novel set during Trujillo's regime in the Dominican Republic and in which torture for political purposes plays a key role. Students will generate questions to deepen their understanding of the issues in the novel and their questions will be used in a Socratic seminar.

Ling-Se Peet was about to use the QFT for the first time with her class. In addition to the challenge of the new practice, she was also aware that these students had their minds on many other things as they neared the end of their high school career, including the prom. These students were success stories in their families, school, and neighborhoods. They had made it through twelve years of schooling—some of them had come as immigrants from Africa and the Caribbean just a few years earlier—and almost all of them were heading off to college, with the majority going to nearby community and commuter colleges.

   Peet knew that they would need some time to think about and discuss the Rules for Producing Questions. "The rules are simple enough," she thought, "but that doesn't mean [my class] is really going to understand how they'll have to behave differently than in our typical classroom discussions. And,this topic, the focus on torture, is not easy."

Indeed, some of her students came from countries where torture is not some abstract concept but an actual practice. For many, it hit too close to home. Would they be able to participate in this process, she wondered, without jumping in with declarations, stopping to discuss, argue, and debate? These were some of the specific issues she faced in introducing the QFT to this class.

Discussing the Rules

Peet's first step was to split the class up into groups of four or five students. Then she passed out a list of the four simple rules. She saw some students quickly put them aside with a shrug that implied, "What's the big deal?" while others looked them over slowly and carefully. She gave them all another moment, then asked, "What might be difficult about following these rules?" and told them to discuss this briefly in their own groups.

This opening small group activity was a dry run of sorts to see how they would manage the discussion on their own. Quickly, and not to her surprise, there were differences in engagement and participation. She heard a couple of students immediately raise concerns related to rule 1 (coming up with as many questions as they could), about not knowing what to ask, but most students focused on the difficult rule 2 not to change, discuss, or judge any questions. Several students went down another common path. One girl said. "I like to answer questions. If I hear a question I like or I'm interested in, I don't wanna wait 'til later to talk about it." A boy in a different group voiced a similar feeling: "I'd wanna get an answer before I move on."

None of the small groups actually got to either rule 3 (write it down exactly as it was stated) or 4 (change every statement into a question). At this point, those rules existed only in the abstract; the students had not yet experienced turning statements into questions. They also had not had much experience changing their own questions or editing and modifying them. The meaning of these rules would become manifest only once they went through the exercise and started to break the rules. At that point, Peet would remind them stick to the rules.

This opening process took about five minutes, concluding with a request for volunteers to share with the entire class what they had talked about in their groups.

Introducing the QFocus

Now it was time for the students to begin producing their own questions. Peet gave each group a sheet of newsprint and a couple of markers. "OK," she announced, "you're about to begin asking your questions. I'm going to give you the QFocus, and the only thing allowed now is asking questions about it." She put on an overhead sheet with big letters:

Torture can be justified

She gave the class a few seconds to absorb these words. When a few hands shot up to ask her, as was usual practice, to explain what she wanted, she just encouraged her students to get started, reminding them, "Follow the Rules for Producing Questions. Just questions now. No discussion!"

Producing the Questions

The groups did produce questions, which are presented here as they were formulated and transcribed by the students.

Group 1: This group comprised four female students—Jasmine, Kandice, Tiffani, and Carmen. Tiffani was the scribe. They got going quickly. As soon as Tiffani wrote down the QFocus at the top of the page, Jasmine started off: "How do you define torture?" This first question put a big issue on the table. The definition of *torture* is one that jurists, legislators, and human rights commissions have grappled with for years. And yet the experts and august bodies have been unable to agree on what can be defined as torture. It was a potent first question that could have provoked a lengthy debate right then, but, keenly aware of the Rules for Producing Questions, the group pressed on.

Carmen asked a second question: "When is torture used?" She was introducing another element here—a push to clarify not only meaning but also context. Then, the questioning went in a different direction when Kandice asked: "Can torture make you happy?"

This caught the other girls by surprise. They sat in silence for a few moments, and then Tiffani came up with: "What justifies torture?" Since she had written down the QFocus, she seemed to take ownership of the words themselves and turned them into a question. She looked satisfied with her question.

Then Jasmine, pushing some of her definitional interests further, wanted to know: "Who are mostly to be tortured?" Then, looking closely at her question as Tiffani wrote it down, she continued: "Do you think torture is an appropriate punishment?"

The group paused at that question, and it looked as if they wanted to begin a debate, but just at that moment, Peet, who was trying to get another group to follow the rules, said to the whole class, "Remember, you're just asking questions here. No discussion." They held off from responding to Jasmine's question. Instead, Tiffani asked: "What do you think they should do to someone who tortures others?" and Jasmine went back to her themes, asking: "In what situations should torture be used?" and quickly following with two more: "Is torture inhumane?" and "Is torture only physical?"

That question prodded Kandice back in the direction of personalizing the implications of torture, but with a different focus: "What are the long-term effects of torture?"

Finally, Tiffani, in a strong voice, asked: "Who should be punished for torture?"

The questions had gone in different directions. If it was still not clear where they were going to go with these questions, it was quite evident that they had used the structure—the Rules for Producing Questions and the process—to accomplish the divergent thinking part of the QFT.

Group 2: This group of two male and two female students—Jerrold, Roland, Tajay, and Danielle—was silent at the outset and seemed to have trouble getting started. Peet noticed that and reminded the class as a whole: "Use the rules and just ask questions. No discussion." As this group saw the other groups getting into the process, they got started. Tajay, the scribe, slowly and deliberate used large block letters to copy the QFocus to the top of the page.

Danielle got them started: "How do you justify torture?" The question seemed to silence them. Roland literally scratched his head and then slowly asked: "What circumstances would require torture?"

They sat again in silence for a bit. Jerrold said, "We can't discuss that?" Tajay, marker in hand, now wondered if that was a question she was supposed to write down. They sat for a while, looking a little frustrated as Peet talked to another group, but then they heard her say, "Just look at the QFocus and keep asking any question that comes to mind." They looked back at their page and the QFocus, and Jerrold, who had wanted to stop to discuss Roland's question, instead asked his own: "Why is torture even effective?"

Danielle followed immediately with: "Is torture done to be a lesson?"

And then Roland got their attention when he asked: "How is torture and justice related?"

Again, the group sat in silence for a few moments contemplating that question. Peet, alert to the fact that other groups had already finished and perhaps assuming that this group's silence meant completion, announced that all groups would need to write down their last question before she moved on to the next step. This got Danielle to ask quickly: "Does the word *can* [in the QFocus) have some special meaning?" Tajay didn't pay much attention to that question, but she wrote it down and then squeezed in one more question of her own: "What effects does torture have on the people being tortured?"

Divergent Thinking by Way of Different Styles, Different Paces, and Different Ideas

It had taken group 2 the full eight minutes Peet had allocated for this step to come up with just seven questions—a contrast to some of the other groups in the room, including one that had produced triple that number. But this step is not a competition to come up with the most questions. It is a process to stimulate, prod, cajole, and engage students in divergent thinking. This group's seven questions were the result of their own divergent thinking efforts. They had heard each other asking about justification for torture, its effectiveness, and its impact on people. They may not have produced a lot of questions, but they got to new places and new ways of thinking related to the QFocus.

The exercise was instructive for Peet as well. She saw that, when given the opportunity to think divergently, groups will go off in different directions and may also explore common themes. Some will do it by producing a lot of questions, others with relatively few. Either way, they are using the process to look closely at the QFocus and unpack the meaning of the terms and ideas presented to them.

When Peet told the class that time was up for this part of the process, the body language in the room had changed. Whereas at the outset students were draped over their chairs in a range of creative ways—some with backs to their peers, some with backs to Peet, and some with a keener focus on a friend or a more intriguing fellow student in a neighboring group, they were now all focused sharply on the paper full of the questions they had produced. They were, as they said later, quite proudly, "our questions." The students had a sense of ownership over those questions and they now demonstrated, at least physically, that they were ready for Peet's instructions about the next step in the process.

Peet noted that she had always thought of her classroom as a student-centered one. But after seeing the way her students responded to the opportunity to generate their own questions, she realized that there is something fundamentally different about students responding to a teacher's question to encourage thinking—no matter how well constructed—versus students getting the chance to generate their own questions. Her students noticed the difference as well.

CASE STUDY: PRODUCING QUESTIONS IN AN URBAN HIGH SCHOOL BIOLOGY CLASS

Teacher: Marcy Ostberg, Boston Day and Evening Academy (a public high school for students who have transferred from other schools or are over age or undercredited)

Subject: Science

Group size: Twelve students working together

QFocus: *Pollution harms Boston residents*

Purpose in using the QFT: Students will be introduced to a subject and will work towards developing a question for an experiment

In Marcy Ostberg's small advanced biology class at the Boston Day and Evening Academy, the students were about to embark on an extended study of *eutrophication* and had spent some time learning the definition: "excessive richness of nutrients in a lake or other body of water, frequently due to runoff from the land, which causes a dense growth of plant life and death of animal life from lack of oxygen."

Ostberg had used the QFT before with this group of students and with others. She thought that it would be good to have them unpack the term and think more deeply about it by using the QFT. Because she had already introduced the Rules for Producing Questions and facilitated a discussion with the students about what might be difficult in following them, she just did a quick review of the rules and asked which rule they had found to be the most difficult to follow. It was an effective way to get the students thinking about the rules again, but from a different perspective—one of experience. A few students talked about having to "beat down," the urge to stop to discuss a question, but, on the whole, they felt quite confident in their use of the rules.

Ostberg started the session off with a very simple QFocus:

Eutrophication

The students' questions, listed below, offer evidence that even the simplest, most barebones QFocus can lead to a divergent thinking process. The original grammatical mistakes are kept; since one of the rules is to "write down each question exactly as it asked," the same should apply to discussing questions "exactly as they were recorded."

1. How does eutrophication occur?
2. How do we avoid eutrophication?
3. Where does eutrophication happen?
4. What impact does eutrophication have on marine animals?
5. What happens when eutrophication occurs?
6. Has eutrophication happen in Boston?
7. What has been done to stop eutrophication?
8. Can eutrophication be rid of?
9. What types of environment does eutrophication occur?
10. What causes cutrophication?
11. Is eutrophication good or essentially bad?
12. Who lives in these marine areas when eutrophication occurs?
13. Is the process of deeutrophication possible?

Given only a quick look, this seems like this is a pretty straightforward list of questions. It's possible to glance at them and move impatiently to thinking about what's next, what did they learn, and what are they going to do with these questions? But before going there, it is important to pause and look more closely at what just happened.

Ostberg was struck simply by the number of questions, noting that she'd "never had students produce so many questions before." This was no small feat, especially for Ostberg's students, who had struggled mightily with critical thinking tasks in school for years (at a similar school in Brooklyn, another teacher was ecstatic to have elicited three questions from a group of students who had not previously written a single word in class).

The order of questions also shows a thinking process more sophisticated than might appear at first glance The first question starts off in a good place, looking for basic information. The second one moves quickly toward action, remediation, and prevention. Then, there's a push for more data, more information about "where" eutrophication happens and its impact on "marine animals."

The sixth question pulls the QFocus closer to home, as students think about the relevance to their own community, while the seventh asks for historical information about the problem and actions taken: "What has been done to stop eutrophication?"

Considering what, if anything, has been done to stop it, produced a new idea: "Can eutrophication be rid of?" This question led to broadened perspectives: if the students were going to be examining ways to get rid of eutrophication, they needed to know more about: "What types of environment does eutrophication occur?"

And then one student realized that they needed to ask a more fundamental question—perhaps the starting question: "What causes eutrophication?" Where had this tenth question been lurking in their brains? What brought it out? How does it inform the previous nine questions?

This question led to another fundamental one that took a step back from some of their assumptions, asking: "Is eutrophication good or essentially bad?" The final two questions deepened and returned to the questions of lives affected and stopping the process: "Who lives in these marine areas when eutrophication occurs?" and "Is the process of deeutrophication possible?

This one set of thirteen questions revealed a divergent thinking process as students took apart the QFocus and thought about different aspects of it as a phenomenon, as a problem, as something in need of response or a solution. The process of turning their blank page into a page full of questions got them thinking in different ways. This is what Ostberg had hoped for when she decided to use the QFT. Even without going on to the next steps, she saw evidence of thinking that was directly related to what she wanted to cover in her next lessons on the topic. As one of the students later said, "Asking questions helps you get straight to the point" and—stating the real value of the QFT—"You are ready to learn more when you've asked the questions yourself."

CASE STUDY: PRODUCING QUESTIONS IN A SUBURBAN MIDDLE SCHOOL SCIENCE CLASS

Teacher: Hayley Dupuy, J. L. Stanford Middle School, Palo Alto, CA
Subject: Science
Group Size: 27 students working in small groups of four to five
QFocus: *Plate tectonics affect geography and communities*
Purpose in using the QFT: Students' questions will shape research and project work for a six week project-based learning unit culminating in presentations to peers and the parent community.

It was a sunny California day in Hayley Dupuy's classroom as twenty-seven sixth-graders streamed in through the one door designated for entrance. The other doors were reserved as exit routes straight to the school's outdoor corridors, an arrangement well suited to California's climate and its location—on top of the San Andreas fault.

The students were just about to think more deeply not only about climate but fault lines through an in-depth study of plate tectonics. Dupuy had prepared to lead them through the QFT in preparation for their upcoming research projects. During the discussion of the rules, one group brought up some unusual observations, talking about how: "It's hard to ask questions you don't already know the answer to" and "It's also hard to not stop to try to get the information or answer to a question that interests you." Dupuy reminded them that they would need to help each other follow the rules and they should choose a recorder for the group. Once they were set, she presented her QFocus:

Plate tectonics affects geography and communities

The six groups seated themselves around small separate tables and went right to work from various starting points. One group wanted to start at the very beginning: "What are plate tectonics?" Another group locked in on two other key words, asking, "How do tectonics *affect geography*? How do tectonics *affect community*? Another group wanted to know "What do they mean by *communities*?" All the groups wound up with lists of between nineteen and twenty-seven questions.

Let's follow one group's process. This group, a mix of boys and girls—Stephanie, Michele, Grace, Liam, Steven, and Daniel—began its journey with a question seeking specific information: How fast do plates move?" That was followed quickly by

"*Why* do plates move?" A couple of questions later, Stephanie embraced a key word from the QFocus and asked: "Do plates affect temperature?"

Including the world *affect* in the question caused the group to take a moment to look more closely at the QFocus. There was silence for a few seconds, and then Liam asked: "Who figured out the answers to all these questions?"

That got some smiles from the group, and they shuffled around a little, shifting body weight, looking up from the newsprint for a moment. Then Michele (she who held the power of the marker) asked a concrete question: "How have plants and animals that live on faults adapted? And, that was followed immediately with "What is the dictionary definition of *plate tectonics*?"

Their "definition" question was the seventh on the list. They continued on through a series of questions about size of volcanoes and animal sensitivity to plate tectonics and then, in question number 14, Daniel asked, "On average, how many people die in earthquakes every year?" The group paused for a moment upon hearing this question, as if out of respect for those victims, then returned to questions about size of plates and how that affects its speed. The originator of question 14 went back to his theme: "On average, how many people are killed by volcanic eruptions every year?"

The group paused again, then shifted back to the emerging interest in speed, animals, and climate. They were twenty questions into the process when Grace, who had remained relatively quiet, looked closely at the QFocus again and asked: "Do plates affect temperature?" This quickly led to: "Do plates affect precipitation?" At that point Dupuy gave the class a one-minute warning to wrap it up and a couple of questions later Stephanie concluded their work with "What animals can sense plates moving?"

It had been a quick, robust production of many questions along a few focused lines of inquiry. The participants both fed off of each other and yet also maintained their own interests as reflected in their questions.

There was a buzz in the room and Dupuy got ready to take that energy and push them a step farther in the process.

TROUBLESHOOTING PRODUCING QUESTIONS

Let's look now at possible challenges you might find while students are working to produce questions and what action to take.

Rule 1: Ask As Many Questions as You Can (Gives License to Ask).   There are a number of potential stumbling blocks related to this rule, including:

- **Students struggle trying to produce the questions:** Give them time to think. Repeat the QFocus and the rules but do not give examples of questions.
- **Students ask for examples:** Do not give examples. Repeat: *Do not give examples.* When you give examples you are setting direction for the questions. Students need to struggle with this a bit. If they are completely stuck, you can use question starters. For example: "You can start a question with words like *what, when,* or *how.* Use one of these words to produce a question about [our QFocus]." Questions starters will be a good strategy for when students are stuck or when they have produced very few questions.
- **Groups are working at different pace:** While some of your small groups will have lots of questions, others will not. This is fine. The work during this exercise should not be judged by the number of questions students produced. If some of your groups are slow in producing questions, just make sure they stay on task by reminding them of the rules.
- **Some students are not participating or one student is producing all the questions:** Remind students about the task and the rules. All group members should contribute questions including the scribe. Remind students of this first rule. All questions are welcomed and valued which will allow the reluctant student to participate.

Rule 2: Do Not Stop to Discuss, Judge, or Answer Any Question (Creates Safe Space and Protection).   Students want to answer a question as it comes up. This rule says it all: do not stop to answer, judge, or discuss. Let students know that there will be opportunities for discussion and addressing the questions in other steps of the process.

Rule 3: Write Down Every Question Exactly as It Is Stated (Levels the Playing Field So All Questions and Voices Are Respected).   Sometimes it will be difficult for the scribe to keep track of the questions and all the words. The challenge is to make sure each question is captured, especially if there's a flurry of questions. Remind students that the whole group is responsible for each question to be written exactly as it was asked. Group members can help the scribe in remembering and recording all the questions.

Change Any Statement into a Question (Insists on the Discipline of Phrasing, Asking, and Thinking in Questions, Not Statement). Potential challenges that may arise with rule 4 include:

- **Students get off task and start talking:** Make sure students stay focused on asking questions. Sometimes you will see students getting off task—talking or discussing. Other times they might think they have asked a question when they have not, using statements or even phrases rather than questions. If you see any of these happening just ask them to change what they were talking about or what the statement they wrote into a question.
- **Students are confused about the instructions:** Confusion could be a result of requesting students to work differently. Repeat the QFocus and the rules to clarify but do not overexplain.
- **The QFocus is not working:** It is important to have a backup plan if the QFocus doesn't work. Plan alternative ways to present the same QFocus. Do not try to explain or give information about the QFocus but give the instructions in a different way: "I want you to ask questions about [alternative QFocus]." Explore with students what is it that they don't understand; this will allow you to restate the instructions in a way they understand.

CONCLUSION

The three teachers whose stories have been told in this chapter, and many others, used the QFT to invite their students to ask questions. They moved well beyond the traditional request "Do you have any questions, or suggestions?" to "Be sure to ask questions about anything you don't understand." In response, their students created a rich tapestry of questions, trailblazed a path in the directions the teachers might never have gotten to on their own, and demonstrated new levels of engagement that matched or exceeded anything the teachers had seen before. The students also learned how to push their thinking with the help of the four Rules for Producing Questions. This experience them to use them on their own, for individual assignments, as well.

But before they consider other applications of what they have just learned, these students will need to go further. They have a list of questions—their own questions, not the teacher's—but it's an unsorted list. The next step is to learn how to make order out of them. The students are about to shift from working hard as divergent thinkers and put new intellectual energy into convergent thinking. They will get to work on making connections, improving their questions, and setting priorities. Now, with their questions on the paper in front of them, they are ready and, in many cases, eager to see what they can do next.

Key Points

The Rules for Producing Questions offer a structure for students to generate their own questions.

Your role is to:

- Facilitate their use of the Rules for Producing Questions.
- Remind students to stick to the rules during the group process.

CHAPTER 5

Students Improve the Questions

Closed- and Open-Ended Questions

*"The Question Formulation Technique gives you an outlet for
further expanding your learning through asking more questions."*

CONSIDER WHAT YOUR STUDENTS HAVE JUST DONE. They worked hard in a
divergent thinking exercise. They may have dedicated more time to questioning and generated more questions than they have ever done. They now have before
them a number of questions that did not exist, nor did they know they were even
in their minds, just a few minutes ago. They are probably champing at the bit to get
answers or to at least know what they are going to do with their questions. But for
now, you are going to put the brakes on that demand.

WHY STOP NOW?

By stopping the momentum for a while, you'll be taking students off the road to
answers to give them another rare opportunity—to transition from a divergent
thinking exercise to a form of convergent thinking. In this step, they will begin to
look more closely at their own questions and take apart what information they can
get from them. To many of them, this may seem like an unnecessary detour because
they are not yet answering the questions. You have to reassure them that the time

will come to get answers, but first they are going to work on creating a path that will lead them far more efficiently to those answers—to look at the differences between *closed-* and *open-ended questions* and to learn how to change one kind into another. The detour, they will eventually see, becomes a shortcut to better answers. And they will also engage in a powerful metacognitive thinking exercise about the purposes and uses of different kinds of questions and ways to obtain information.

Just knowing the difference between closed- and open-ended questions does not mean that students have internalized all possible distinctions between questions. The work on distinguishing kinds of questions, different purposes, forms, and goals can go on for a long time. Questions can be classified as being of different types and for different purposes; for information gathering, analysis, synthesis, evaluation, and comprehension. They can be classified as higher- or lower-order, thick or thin, factual, rhetorical, hypothetical, etc. But spending too much time learning too many types of questions can undermine the deep learning that takes place when students put most of their energy into the production and analysis of their own questions. Students who learn the differences between closed- and open-ended questions climb a sharp learning curve in a very small amount of time. We have seen in many settings that it is a transformative moment when the student discovers and truly understands this one important lesson: *The construction and phrasing of a question shapes the kind of information you can expect to receive.*

For some students who are learning about closed- and open-ended questions for the first time, this is an exciting and profound discovery. Many who are already familiar with the distinction find that paying closer attention and gaining experience in changing the questions helps them develop a far keener sense of question production, information gathering, and analytical thinking.

INTRODUCING CLOSED- AND OPEN-ENDED QUESTIONS

The process for teaching students about closed- and open-ended questions is simple and straightforward (see table 5.1). Your role in this part is to introduce the definition of closed-ended and open-ended questions, facilitate the discussion about the questions, and support students as they work on changing their questions from one kind to another.

TABLE 5-1

Teacher and student roles in discussion; closed- and open-ended questions

Teacher role	Student role
• Introduce a definition for closed- and open-ended questions.	• Review list of questions they have produced.
	• Categorize questions as closed- or open-ended.
• Support students as they categorize questions.	
• Facilitate a discussion on the advantages and disadvantages of closed- and open-ended questions.	• Name advantages and disadvantages of asking closed- and open-ended questions.
• Support students as they work on changing questions from one type to another.	• Practice changing questions from closed- to open-ended and from open- to closed-ended.

The process for working with closed- and open-ended questions takes between seven and ten minutes the first time students are introduced to the QFT process. After that, this step should take around five minutes . This part of the process offers flexibility on which parts of the exercise to use once students have been introduced to all the steps. The process can develop as follows.

1. Provide a definition for closed- and open-ended questions:
   - A *closed-ended question* is answered with a one-word response such as yes or no or another single word. *Example:* Is this going to be on the test?
   - An *open-ended question* requires more explanation. *Example:* What will be on the test?

   These definitions provide students with clear criteria that help them begin to differentiate between a bunch of questions that seem to run together. It is useful to post a chart, as shown in figure 5.1, with the definition and advantages and disadvantages for easy review.

2. Instruct students to review the list of questions they produced and mark closed-ended questions with a "C" and open-ended with an "O." Two to three minutes will be enough time to complete this task.

3. Facilitate a discussion on the advantages and disadvantages of closed- and open ended questions. You will need about four minutes for this discussion, depending on what strategy you use. Students can discuss advantages and disadvantages in small groups that will report their conclusions, or as a large group.

FIGURE 5.1

Advantages and disadvantages of closed- and open-ended questions

Closed-ended questions Answered with yes/no or one word answer		Open-ended questions Need an explanation	
Advantages	*Disadvantages*	*Advantages*	*Disadvantages*

4. Instruct students to change questions from one type to another. You decide on the number of questions they change. Changing one or two questions is enough for practice. It will take about three minutes to complete this task.

The following case study illustrates the process.

CASE STUDY: WHAT HAPPENS WHEN STUDENTS WORK ON CATEGORIZING QUESTIONS AS CLOSED- AND OPEN-ENDED

In Marcy Ostberg's high school biology class, the students in one small group of four had generated a healthy list of twelve questions from her QFocus:

Evolution of the eye

She first offered the quick, minimalist definition of both kinds of questions described in item 1 above, and set forth what seemed like a simple task: marking the questions as closed- or open-ended.

The students looked at the first one on the list: "How did the eye evolve?" That one was easy; they put a large "O" next to it. Then they looked at the second one: "When did the eye evolve?" There was some hesitation. One student said, "Well, that doesn't have a one-word answer." but another countered: "Yeah, but if there is a definite time when it evolved, isn't that like a one-word answer? Doesn't that make it closed?" Ostberg heard this debate, but stayed out of the discussion. The students decided to mark it "O/C," meaning that it could be either or both.

The difficulty of the categorization continued with their next question: "What are the parts of the eye?" They debated some more. "There are a bunch of one-word answers to this question. Does that make it a kind of closed-ended question?" They weren't quite sure, so they asked Ostberg to adjudicate for them. She told them that sometimes it's not completely clear whether it is open or closed so they should just do the best they could. They marked it with a "C."

Then, they got to their next question: "How do [the parts] work?" There was an audible sigh of relief. They talked about how this question would "require more explanation" so they confidently put an "O" next to it. They got more energized as they went down the rest of their list and felt clearer and more confident about how to categorize their questions:

- **Why does the eye have different parts?** Without hesitation, That's open!
- **Do some animals have different eyes than others?** That's closed!
- **What is the difference between human eyes and animal eyes?** Hesitation. Is there a one-word answer to this question, or does it require more explanation? They voted for "more explanation" and marked it with an "O."
- **Why do some people say it's not possible for the eye to have evolved?** A big—very big—*why* question. No doubt, said one of the students, that's an open-ended question.
- **Why are eye colors different from each other and how would that have formed?** No hesitation. They put an "O" by it (and noticed that this one question should have been split up into two separate ones).

Then the group looked at the next question: "What were some of the transitions in eye evolution?" They slowed down a bit, wondered again if this was asking for a couple of one-word answers or if there would be something more involved in answering the question. By this time, comfortable with the existence of a grey area between the two categories, they marked it "O/C."

They marked their final three questions on the list with confidence and relief:

- Were there other theories for how the eye evolved?—C
- Is the eye a single cell?—C
- How does the eye function?—O

What had just happened? The students had dedicated a solid block of time and great intellectual energy to looking closely at a list of questions. And not just any list of questions—it was a list of questions *they* had generated. They spent time trying to categorize the questions and considering what kind of information each question would elicit. They were examining closely how and whether the wording of the question might affect or even change the information that would come in the form of an answer. They were, according to Marcy Ostberg, "more engaged than I think I have ever seen them."

Ostberg could also hear the quality of discussion and the depth of thinking evident in the different groups. But in order for the students to recognize the full power of what they had just done, they needed a chance to name all that themselves, in their own words. That's the purpose and the metacognitive value of the next step: *Asking the students to consider the advantages and disadvantages of both kinds of questions.*

DISCUSSING ADVANTAGES AND DISADVANTAGES FOR EACH TYPE OF QUESTION

Once your students have categorized their questions, they will have paid unusually close attention to the characteristics of two kinds of questions. They will have struggled with questions that don't fit easily into just one category or another. This is serious work, not unlike the hard intellectual labor of linguists and philosophers struggling with words and the various meanings and interpretations.

Now, you are about to give them a chance to reflect on and name what they had learned in the process. You ask them first: "What are some advantages of a closed-ended question?"

The students may give a look of "Come again?" for since, if they are already familiar with the notion of closed- and open-ended questions, then they will have internalized one message from many teachers: Open-ended questions are "better" questions. It is a shock to many to be asked to think about the advantages to the closed-ended questions. For those students who are learning about the differences for the first time, your question to them seems neutral enough; no hint of cognitive dissonance.

Because you are building students' ability to distinguish and then think about the different uses of the questions, it is important to offer the positive option—to contemplate the advantages first. There may be a moment of hesitation but then they may offer comments such as these about closed-ended questions:

- They're quick.
- They get you clear information right away.
- You get a very specific answer.

After you hear some of these responses and while some students (who were sure just a moment ago that there are no advantages to a closed-ended question) are just absorbing their meaning, you follow with another question to the group as a whole: "What are some disadvantages of closed-ended questions?" The responses come even more quickly now:

- They don't give you much information.
- They close off discussion.
- You don't learn what you really want to know.
- You may need to know more or you want more information but all you got was a one-word answer.

Back on safe ground, students are now ready for the next question: "What are some advantages of open-ended questions?" They are prepared for this one.

- You get more information.
- You find out more.
- You get a fuller explanation.
- It will give you more information.
- You get to hear what the other person is thinking.
- You might get an explanation that helps you understand more.

But then, just as they are back in their comfort zone, repeating what they've heard many times before, they're tripped up by the final question: "What are some disadvantages of open-ended questions?" There's a hesitation, and then the acknowledgment begins:

- You may get too much information.
- You get the runaround.
- You may not get the information you need.
- And you don't understand everything being told to you.
- You don't understand the answer or know what to do with it.
- You can be more confused.
- It can be too long.

As a closing to the discussion on advantages and disadvantages, you can summarize students' comments, pointing out that there is value in knowing the difference between closed- and open-ended questions and that *both* types of questions are useful. There are times in which an open-ended question is what is needed and other times a closed-ended is what works best.

CHANGING THE QUESTIONS FROM ONE TYPE TO ANOTHER

You will now offer your students a chance to build on their knowledge of the differences between closed- and open-ended questions. They will have the chance to develop a robust ability to change a question from one category into another.

The instructions you give are simple and concise. You will ask students to choose at least one of their closed-ended questions and change it to an open-ended question, and then to take at least one open-ended question and change it to a closed-ended question.

Students may struggle a bit in this process. They are still climbing a very sharp learning curve as they discuss among themselves how to turn a question into something that will require more than a yes-or-no answer. They might struggle as well when they try to take an open-ended question and narrow it down to insure they get a closed answer.

Learning About Question Starters

You can offer to the class as a whole a quick view of different question starters such as:

- Open-ended questions start with *Why?* and *How?*
- Closed-ended questions start with *Is?*, *Do?*, and *Can?*
- Words that could be used for both types of questions: *What?*, *Who?*, *Where?*, and *When?*

Because some questions can go into one or the other category, it is helpful to remind students that the key is to think about the limits and extent of information they can get from their questions. One teacher used student questions to illustrate the differences between questions that can go into different categories, for example:

- *Who is the president?* A one-word specific answer, versus *Who is qualified?* The second question can be responded to literally (e.g., thirty-five years old, native-born citizen of the United States) or can be interpreted as *What is your opinion on who among the candidates is qualified?* or *Who should be considered quali-fied to be president?*
- *When does the student council meet?* versus *When would be some good times for the student council to meet?*
- *When can we ask questions at the public hearing?* (specific answer) versus *When would it be most effective for us to ask questions?*

It is a judgment call on when in the process to provide question starters. Too soon, and you wind up shaping the questions the students ask. Too late and they may have gotten stuck or confused. Some confusion is good. Too much is generally not. That distinction is probably familiar to you. We have seen that it is generally better for students to struggle with this on their own—to try to explain why they believe one question is open or closed—and let them learn from peers in their own groups and from other groups about how they have named and changed their questions. If there is a need to explain, clarify, or give assistance, you should do this only after they have tried to do it on their own, not before.

In Marcy Ostberg's science class, students pushed and probed their own think-ing as they began the process for changing their questions. They looked at their open-ended question, "What is the difference between human eyes and animal eyes?" They realized that there was an assumption built into that question (raised assertively by one student who asked, "How do you know that's even true?!"). They agreed they needed to start off with a more basic question and found it helpful to change the open-ended question into a closed-ended one: "Are there differences between human and animal eyes?"

Then they set out to change a closed-ended question into an open-ended one. They looked at this question: "Were there other theories for how the eye evolved?" Using what they had learned about question starters, they played around with the opening words *how* and *why*. One student asked, "How did the eye evolve?" But another noticed that there was nothing in that question about theories." One of the students suggested using the word *what* and then asked: "What are the theories for how the eye came to be?" They agreed that this wording gave them a different way to look at the question, "a better way," as one of the students noted.

In classroom after classroom, students and teachers report that knowing the difference between the two kinds of questions and being able to change one to another has a major impact on them. When asked what they have learned, the students state it very clearly:

- I learned the difference between closed- and open-ended questions.
- I now know how to change questions from one kind to another.
- I need to think about how I ask my question.
- I see that I can get different information based just on how I ask the question. I never knew that before.

The cognitive change—knowing the difference—and the behavioral change—transforming the questions—produces an affective change as well. Students talk about how being able to change the questions makes them feel more confident about working with questions and figuring out how to solve problems for themselves. Teachers notice the difference as well. Yana Minchenko, at the Boston Day and Evening Academy, works with students who have frequently felt powerless in their lives and in their experiences in school. The exercise in changing the questions turns out to be an experience in taking some power for themselves. As Minchenko notes:

> Students gain power by the ability to manipulate the questions . . . I think it gives them a sense of power that they usually lack in their learning. The idea that they *can* change questions makes them see things differently. I've seen them [taking] the markers—that too gives them a sense that they are the ones doing the work—and marking the closed- and open-ended questions and scratching out one version and

replacing it with another. One girl had her head on the table, but when it was time to mark the questions, all of a sudden she sat up straight, took the marker, and became very active. There's something about it that energizes them.

Three Options for a Next Step

At this point you have three options for a next step:

1. **Relate the categories of questions to a purpose:** If you have a very specific purpose in mind for how you want students to use their questions at the end of the process, you may want to relate the categories of questions to that purpose. For example, if you want them to design a laboratory experiment, at this stage you may want them to think about—before they move on to the prioritization step—what kinds of questions are used in different stages of an experiment. They may need to think about how they would use both closed- and open-ended questions. If you want them to design a research project, you may want them to think about why they may want to use an open-ended question rather than a closed-ended question as their overarching question.

2. **Continue straight on to prioritizing the questions:** If you are using the QFT to introduce a new subject or to assess what students understand from work already done, then you may not want to do any further work on closed- and open-ended questions but instead move them to the next step in the process—prioritization.

3. **Create lists of situations in which these types of questions would be appropriate:** You can work with the class on creating a list of situations or purposes when it would make sense to use open-ended questions or to use closed-ended questions. This can be an ongoing project that will continuously attune the students to thinking about what information they need and how to use their new ability to formulate their own questions to their best advantage.

No matter which of these options you choose, you will want to acknowledge the students' observations about the advantages and disadvantages of both kinds of questions. You will want to be sure that they hear from you that:

- There is value to both kinds of questions.
- There are times when one kind may be more helpful than another.
- It is important to be able to change a question from one kind to another.

- It can be helpful to change the question from one to another as a way to look at the issue in a fresh way.

TROUBLESHOOTING ASKING CLOSED- AND OPEN-ENDED QUESTIONS

As students learn to first categorize the types of questions and then to change them from one to the other, you may have to help them overcome the following challenges:

There Is Disagreement on Categorizing a Question. Sometimes students will debate how to categorize a question or will disagree about how a question was categorized. One student may say it is closed-ended while others think it is open-ended. In this situation it could be that the categorization is wrong or that the question can fit in both categories. When this happens in small groups, students know that they have limited time for discussion and usually mark the question as "C/O"—both closed and open. You will even see that sometimes during group reports students will disagree on how a question was categorized. You don't need to discuss this likelihood ahead of time, since debate will likely deepen thinking. But you can help students learn to categorize the questions by:

- Asking them to think about the kinds of answers they can get from asking the question
- Using question starters:
  - *Why, what, how*—Open-ended
  - *When, where, who, is, can, do*—Closed-ended

Changing the Questions—The New Question Is Not Related to the Original Students soon discover that it is easy to change questions from one type to another by just changing one word. But sometimes the changed question means something different or is not related to the original one. The value of working to change the types of questions is that students learn to distinguish the differences and to change the questions. Do not worry too much about different meaning, but do make students *aware* that the new question means something different. You can also ask students to think about a new question that is closer to the original one.

CONCLUSION

The most important principle for your students to internalize for the long term is the following: *The construction and phrasing of a question shapes the kind of information you can expect to receive.*

The work students have done on categorizing and changing their questions can be challenging, but generally not intimidating. They have done a great deal of hard thinking, but they were working on a very concrete, very specific task. There were just two categories to keep in mind. They were not starting, as they did before, with a blank sheet of paper—an imposing task. Rather, they started from what they had already produced. And, you, as their teacher, gave them very specific guidelines for doing the work. To some extent, they were working back in familiar and comfortable territory.

The next step, however, will push them harder and deeper into new territory. They are about to take on a challenging but often overlooked thinking ability: prioritization.

Key Points

- There are advantages and disadvantages in producing both closed- and open-ended questions.
- Students need to have a full discussion on closed- and open-ended questions the first time they are introduced to the QFT. After that, you can choose which parts of the closed and open-ended exercise to complete. For example, you do not need to discuss advantages and disadvantages every time you use the process. You might decide to ask students to categorize the questions as closed or open and stop there, or you might ask them to find an example of each type of question and change it.
- Students often describe the work on closed- and open-ended questions as an exercise of discovery, new knowledge and awareness, and also fun.

CHAPTER 6

Students Prioritize the Questions

Analysis and Convergence

*"I've found that asking questions helps me think more
deeply about the topic we are looking at. I get more information
out of a document if I ask myself questions about it."*

W**HEN DO WE LEARN TO PRIORITIZE?** How do we learn it? How does it affect our chances for learning and performing effectively across different subjects and environments if we never quite learn to prioritize?

The ability to prioritize may be one of the most important—yet too often overlooked—skills that a student can acquire in their formal education. You have probably seen your students come up with their own ideas or gather information about a topic from a slew of sources, only to struggle mightily to make sense of all of it. Your experiences and your knowledge about how to organize an essay, design an experiment, and carry out a research project, allow you to quickly see what is central to the task and what may be tangential; your students, however, may not know how to even begin to rank the order and value of what they see in front of them.

This is the point in the QFT when you are about to help them begin developing the ability to prioritize. You will be challenging them to test and strengthen yet another thinking muscle. Unlike the "question-asking muscle" that atrophied over the years since early childhood, the "prioritization muscle" has never had a chance to develop. Recent research shows that the part of the brain most needed for wise decision-making—certainly informed by an ability to prioritize—is not fully developed in adolescence.[1] Your students will need more chances to strengthen that muscle and part of the brain, not just for the classroom, but as a lifelong skill.

It is a good moment to challenge them. They are riding a wave of satisfaction with what they have done. They've used a structured process and the Rules for Producing Questions and have successfully produced more questions than they may have thought they could ever generate. They've carefully examined them. They've categorized them as best they could as closed-and open-ended questions and practiced changing questions from one type to another. This is already a serious amount of work. Your students are, as they will tell you later, already aware of having learned something new and of having deepened their understanding of the topic and of the value and purpose of different kinds of questions.

They will now take on a challenge that has bedeviled many people inside of education and beyond. The act of prioritization—the ability to assign importance properly is an intellectual task involving a wide range of skills, including comparison, categorization, analysis, assessment, and synthesis. Getting prioritization right can be a challenging and trying process and, as many of the world's greatest scientists have discovered, you might, at first, still get it wrong.[2]

Prioritization may be one of the greatest thinking challenges your students face in their own lives every day. They have to prioritize and make decisions related to their use of time in and out of class, online and offline, with peers, in their environment, and in their daily engagement with short-term and long-term schoolwork. They have to prioritize all the time, but because they do not use a deliberate process for it nor consciously practice it, they do not necessarily acquire the ability to see the steps they need to take and the criteria they need to develop in order to do it effectively. Giving your students the chance to practice a prioritization process and use their own handiwork—their questions—will sharpen their ability to analyze opinions and make decisions. This step in the QFT gives them the opportunity to practice the act and art of prioritization. It is not a mastered discipline when done once, or twice, or several times. It is an ability that develops through trial and error and much experience.

You are helping your students move along on that journey and they will be doing it with the questions they now own—that is, their own questions.

THE PROCESS FOR SELECTING THE PRIORITY QUESTIONS—A BASIC OVERVIEW

Students continue working in the same groups in which they categorized the questions. They will need about five minutes to prioritize. The process can develop as follows:

1. Students prioritize by choosing three questions from their list; choices are based on criteria you have established, for example:
   - Choose the three *most important* questions.
   - Choose the three questions that *most interest you.*
   - Choose the three questions that will best help you *design your research project.*
   - Choose the three questions that will *move students toward the purpose of using the QFT.*
2. Students choose three priority questions as follows:
   - First, review the list of questions and quickly discuss which ones to choose.
   - Second, get to an agreement. Choose by consensus, voting, or any other strategy.
3. Students explain their reasons for choosing the three priority questions.
4. Students discuss the reasons among themselves and prepare to explain them to the large group.
5. Small groups report their priority questions and rationale for choosing them to the larger group.

Because prioritization can be a challenging task, pushing students to analyze, assess, compare, contrast and, most of all, reach some kind of agreement on three priority questions, will be the most challenging part of the QFT for you to facilitate. You will have to lean on your full set of skills for encouraging independent thinking, keeping a handle on helping group processes move along without too much direction from you.

SETTING CLEAR CRITERIA FOR PRIORITIZATION

Before the process begins, you will need to set clear, but not overly prescriptive criteria for prioritization. The criteria should be related to your original purpose, the design of the QFocus, and where you are going with your next steps. For example, your goals for what they will do next with their questions could be:

- Writing an essay
- Research
- Developing a project
- Making a presentation
- Class discussion
- Independent study
- Reading a book or article

The criteria for choosing priority questions should be kept as simple as possible, for example:

- What students would like to focus on
- What is most important to students
- What the students can explore further
- What students can use for a specific purpose: conducting an experiment, writing a paper, reading a book

STEPS IN THE PRIORITIZATION PROCESS

As you lead your students through the prioritization process, you'll be following these steps.

Giving Directions for Prioritization

The basic instruction for the prioritization exercise is: *Choose three questions*. After that, the directions you give should be influenced by what you want students to start doing once they have finished the question formulation process. Look at these examples of how teachers have directed students to prioritize and consider the difference between these instructions:

- Choose the three *most important* questions.
- Choose the three questions *you want/need to answer first*.
- Choose the three questions that *most interest you*.

Each directive provides many opportunities for students to choose their three questions without offering an inkling of what *the teacher* might choose as a priority question. And each option is just open enough and just focused enough to allow for student thinking while setting some purpose and direction. There also may be a need to narrow the directions further. Consider, for example, students who need to design an experiment. They may benefit from one of the instruction options above, or they may need something like:

- Choose the three questions that could *help you design your experiment.*
- Choose three *testable* questions.

If students need to write a research paper, the directions might include the first three above or might go directly to:

- Choose the three questions that could *help you come up with a research topic.*
- Choose the three questions that could *help you narrow your research focus.*
- Choose the three questions that *you could start to research* immediately.

The basic instructions are the same. The modifications are based on the purpose of the QFT—the next steps the class will be doing.

Choosing Priority Questions

To choose the three priority questions, students will first review the list of questions and then discuss them quickly. They can use a variety of strategies, which you can decide ahead of time. For example: choose by voting; have each group member choose a question and tally the choices; or discuss and reach group consensus. This discussion can take time. Make sure to let your students know how much time they have to complete the task.

Students Provide a Rationale for the Priority Questions

Next, students discuss among themselves the reasons for selecting their three priority questions. They will need to come up with a rationale for their choices. This is a very important part in the process because it helps students review and think carefully about why they see some questions as more important, more promising, more relevant, or more urgent than others. They learn a lot from each other in this discussion, and it prepares them to listen more attentively to the priority questions from the other groups.

Students Report Their Work

After the groups have chosen their questions, the small groups report the following information to the large group in this sequence:

1. Closed- and open-ended questions they changed (reporting the original and the changed one)
2. Priority questions they chose
3. Rationale for choosing those as priority questions.

You can keep this part very simple or use some other strategies for reporting you practice in your classroom. One spokesperson reports, other group members add their comments. Group members report different parts of the exercises they completed.

CASE STUDY: STUDENTS PRIORITIZING QUESTIONS IN AN URBAN HIGH SCHOOL

As we saw in chapter 4, Ling-Se Peet's QFocus, "Torture can be justified," was a catalyst for a long list of questions. The groups had worked on changing some of their closed-ended questions to open-ended ones and vice versa. Now, they had to choose three priority questions from their list.

Peet didn't share, for the moment, that she would use the questions to guide an upcoming Socratic Seminar. She first wanted to see what they would choose without having to think about the seminar structure. She asked them to choose what they considered to be the most important questions.

Though "Prioritize your questions" sounds like just one more simple step, it is an important step that cannot be skipped, because it moves students from that undifferentiated—*unjudged*—mass of questions they came up with earlier at the beginning of the process toward a sharper focus and positions them to take action and use their questions strategically. This next logical step requires complex decision making that will tax and challenge students' thinking and their ability to work in a group.

Groups Work on Prioritizing Questions

It was fascinating to observe the groups at work. One of the groups discussed in chapter 4—Jasmine, Kandice, Tiffani, and Carmen—had created what philosophers would recognize as epistemological questions about the definition, meaning, and limits of torture. The act of producing questions had drawn them in, and they did not relate to torture as an abstract concept or one that is distant from their lives. As they began their discussion on how to prioritize the questions, they pushed and challenged each other to make a case for their preferences.

Jasmine argued for her question, "How do you define torture?" "You have to first know what we're talking about. If you don't know what it means, you can't judge it," she said quite emphatically.

The four girls kept looking at the list of questions. No one seemed to want to touch Kandice's question, "Can torture make you happy?" Going further down the list, Kandice, apparently eager to move the group's attention to other questions, added: "I like your question, Tiffani, about what justifies torture." Tiffani let a slight smile appear, but then said: "Well, but now I'm thinking about it differently because of this question," and she pointed to the ninth question: "In what situations should torture be used?"

They started to talk about the *should* in that question. Did it mean then that torture *can* be justified? They were starting to think and discuss in questions and came to a difficult juncture: "Well," Carmen piped in, "if we make that a priority question, does that mean that we're agreeing that torture can be justified? What do we do then with number 5 ('What justifies torture?')?"

They were stumped for a moment. Kandice offered, "Maybe we should look at the other ones."

Jasmine said: "That question—number 12—about if 'torture is only physical' makes me think about it. It gets harder to just think about one easy definition."

Kandice, back on firm ground, said, "Look at number 6: 'Who are mostly to be tortured?' We changed that to 'Are younger or older people mostly tortured?' I want to know that." She was pushing for a prioritization that allowed her to get some definite answers, even while Jasmine was struggling with the initial step of naming, identifying, defining and establishing the boundaries around what constitutes the act of torture.

Tiffani listened to Kandice, and said: "If you get tortured when you are young then that could stay with you for a long time, just like number 13 asks: "What are the long-term effects of torture?"

That observation got full agreement from the whole group; they definitely wanted to know the answer to "Are younger or older people mostly tortured?"

Peet was telling the groups to wrap up their prioritization and get ready to report to the whole class when Carmen, who had caught the tension between questions earlier made a pitch for "What justifies torture?" She maintained, "We need to know that if we're going to be thinking about it more." They seemed to have moved past a burning desire to define the term and agreed to that as a second priority question. Somehow, agreeing on that question also pushed them to accept that torture happens, so, Tiffani said, thinking back to her concern about the long-term effects, "Let's make [the last question] a priority: "Who should be punished for torture?"

On the other side of the room, the group made up of Jerrold, Tajay, Roland, and Danielle was having a spirited discussion. They had been quiet and deliberate in the question production stage and had only produced seven in total. The prioritization process, in contrast, triggered some boisterous discussion.

Danielle liked her question that had started them off: "How do you justify torture?" Roland countered, "Well, that's why I asked my question next: 'What circumstances would require torture?' Because you need to look at what specific reasons you might have, that's *how* you can justify it. But, first you gotta explain the circumstances."

Danielle jumped in: "Yeah, like what if it's a terrorist or they're going to do something and you gotta find out. Those are reasons people justify torture."

"Yeah," Jerrold acknowledged, "but how do you know that torture is even effective? That's why I think we have to make that question—the one about 'Why is torture even effective?' one of our priority ones."

No one made mention of Danielle's question about the role and significance of the word *can* in the QFocus. Danielle didn't bring it up, but she did make a case for another question she had asked: "Is torture done to be a lesson?" She noted, "Sometimes, it's used to try to keep other people from doing stuff." Tajay, already thinking on that path, responded with: "That's what they say about the death penalty. But, you really think anyone about to kill someone gonna stop and say 'wait a minute, I'm not doing it because they kill me?' That don't stop no one."

Danielle seemed persuaded and went back to the very last question on the list: "What effects does torture have on the people being tortured?" Roland stayed away from the question he had asked about how torture and justice are related and went along with the group's focus on the effectiveness of torture. "People be getting punished all the time," he said, "maybe that's why they think they need to do torture, for it to be a lesson to them."

Jerrold went back to the question "Why is torture even effective?" and said: "Let's change that to [the new question he had raised as part of the discussion]: "How do you know that torture is even effective?" Tajay, either done with writing or just because she thought this violated the rules, yelled out: "Ms. Peet. Ms. Peet! Can we be changing questions and writing new ones?"

Peet answered, "Well, if it came up as part of your discussion and you want to make it a priority question, that's all right. You're now trying to choose what you think are the three most important questions you can ask about this."

Jerrold looked more that a little satisfied while Tajay seemed irritated, and grudgingly wrote the question down. Danielle said, "All right, which ones we got now? We gotta choose three."

When Peet told the class to start wrapping up, the group looked at their list again. Tajay, having made peace with the change, actually said, "Well, she [Ms. Peet] said we can use this [new one on the effectiveness of torture] and it is kinda better than the other ones. I mean, if you don't know if it even has an effect on someone, you can't be justifying it." Danielle, on terra firma when focused on specifics, wanted them to include "Is torture done to be a lesson?"

The group accepted that but hesitated on the third choice. They heard one more reminder from Peet to wrap up, and Jerrold then said: "Well, I think that question [that Roland had asked] on how they be related, torture and justice, is something we gotta think more about. I'm not saying it's the most important one, but we need to think more about that." Getting to choose three questions, rather than one, gave them the latitude to include it. They agreed and finished.

Groups Report to Each Other

When all the groups reported their prioritized questions, the two groups just described responded in two distinct ways. Sometimes they heard questions they hadn't thought of at all and reacted physically, with sounds and signs of approval and appreciation. The groups were struck by the different phrasing and angles of others' priority questions, in particular:

- How can someone's pain be the price for the outcome you want?
- Who decides whether it should be justified or not?

Then, there was another response mode. They would hear a question that was similar to their own and then "reconvene," talking animatedly among themselves about "that's just like/kinda like the one we asked!" Danielle, for one, responded strongly to a group's priority question:

- Why does torture work?

And they all liked hearing another question that resonated strongly with their own:

- Does justice have anything to do with torture?

When this happened, Peet called for their attention and asked that they listen to all the questions until the reports were finished. Some students nodded their heads approvingly of what they had done. Some looked spent, having just done a lot more thinking then they had expected to do when they walked into class that day.

And it was a lot of thinking. They had just climbed a steep incline on their learning curve. They used their own questions to debate, discuss, assess, and prioritize. They had produced all those questions and then they had to make decisions about which ones were the most important. In their prioritization discussions, points had been made that were not so different from those debated in Congressional committee meetings and Supreme Court deliberations. The students had set their own agenda: they wanted to know about the justification for torture, its effectiveness, its impact on people, and who was more likely to be tortured and why. They had asked questions related to a sense of right and wrong, and pressed hard to know what could justify its use.

In a very short time they had traveled a great intellectual distance, starting off with an intensive burst of divergent thinking and then, step by step, moving along a convergent thinking process, categorizing their questions. Then they had tackled the hard intellectual labor of analyzing and prioritizing and, in the process, needed to find a way to persuade their peers to choose certain questions as the priority ones.

CASE STUDY: DISCOVERING A PRIORITY QUESTION IN A MIDDLE SCHOOL SCIENCE CLASS

In the sixth grade science class in Palo Alto that we met in chapter 4. Ms. Dupuy's students were engaged in the same kind of give and take as they were prioritizing questions around the QFocus: "Plate tectonics affect geography and communities." In their case, Hayley Dupuy explained to her students that they would be choosing a priority question that they would put up on the board along with one priority question from each of the other groups.

It was an interesting variation on the "choose three priority" questions strategy that is often used. Dupuy told the class that once all the priority questions were on the board, they could then pick one they'd be interested in exploring further as they went on to concentrate on a specific geographic location and examine how plate tectonics affects that location and its communities. She gave the groups ten minutes to choose their priority question, knowing that they'd need a little more time than usual to get it down to one question.

The group that had shown an interest in animal behavior and loss of life related to plate tectonics, as well as consequences for climate, started debating their questions. They were very strategic in their analysis of the relative value of the questions. They also continued asking questions as part of their process for ranking the list of questions they had come up with.

"Which ones can be answered easily?" asked Liam, to which, Stephanie responded: "Yeah, it doesn't make sense to spend a lot of time in the project thinking about those questions."

Michele, who held the marker, responded to the prioritization challenge as though she had just been given a thirty-second window to strike through and rule out all basic factual questions. She went at it with gusto. But, she ran into opposition when she tried to strike out this question: "How come there are volcanoes not on faults?" Daniel said, "Hey, wait! That's not so simple." "That's an open question," he insisted, comfortable with his understanding now of both closed- and open-ended questions. The group debated that for a while until Michele conceded, and said, "OK, fine. Let's look at any others we can rule out."

No one seemed too interested in finding out, on average or not, how many people die in earthquakes. They were more sharply focused now on thinking about a question that could be interesting and productive to explore during the next few weeks. They went back to the QFocus and the recorder underlined the word *affect*; one of the boys pressed, "We had questions on that. Where are they?"

They scanned the list. Look at this one, Michele said, number 18: "Does the size of a plate affect its thickness?" "Yeah, well, that's a closed-ended one," said Steven. "We're not going to get much from that. I don't want to spend a lot of time on that." Then, they saw these next two questions (which were actually numbers 21 and 22 on their list out of a total of twenty-four questions):

1. "How do plates affect temperature?"
2. "Do plates affect precipitation?"

"This is really what we should be talking about," Michele asserted. "Yeah, but, which one?" asked Daniel, who had previously asked the questions about average deaths.

"Well," Michele started, putting the previous discussion to use, "the open-ended one makes sense here because we're going to need to work on it for a while." She got agreement on "How do plates affect temperature?" and they looked particularly proud as they pointed out that it was the question they had changed from closed-ended—"Do plates affect temperature?"—to the final open-ended version.

TROUBLESHOOTING PRIORITIZING QUESTIONS

Below are some examples of methods teachers have used to address teaching challenges that can arise during the prioritization process.

Students Cannot Agree on Questions

- **Must there always be three priority questions?** *No.* Your students discover many things along the way just by trying to choose three priority questions. But, what if, as they are thinking convergently, they can't find three they like, or can only agree on two, or want to include a fourth? What should you do?

  It depends, in part, on what you want to happen next, but it is fine to be flexible with the number. It is fine if you prefer they choose just one. If they are excited about four and can't let go of one, that can work. The key point is for them to do the convergent thinking that winnows down their list from a bunch of questions and having a smaller number of questions is more manageable. Also, you may want a group or class to eventually get to one question, depending on the next steps you have planned. You can stagger that process—choose three at first, and after that choose one from that list of three.

- **Students cannot agree on which questions to choose as a group:** Sometimes the groups will have challenges in getting to an agreement and there are different opinions. When this happens you can use a different strategy, such as students individually choose the questions or teams of two choose the questions. They can report their questions individually or the questions can be tallied to find the priority questions.
- **Students cannot agree on why they chose the priority questions:** As you are monitoring and supporting the group work, make sure students complete this part. If they are unable to reach consensus as a group about why they chose a question, ask for volunteers from the group to react to the questions they chose and how they arrived to their priority questions.

Teacher Role

- **Supporting students as they prioritize:** Do not try to model or suggest priority questions. This may set direction for which questions to choose. Support students by reminding them of the criteria for choosing.
- **Faciliting small group reports:** These are brief reports that should not take a lot of time. The purpose is for students to learn from each other how they approached the same QFocus from different perspectives. Small groups usually assign a volunteer to report or they may report in collaboration or you can decide how you want to structure the reports. You can also give additional instructions to help students focus during the reports. For example, "You may want to see if there are questions that are similar to yours."
- **Validating students' contributions during reports:** The reporting part is an important step in the process. It is here that some students gain the confidence to participate more actively in class. It helps students and classroom dynamics when you validate all student contributions equally. Putting more value in some contributions than in others can discourage participation. A simple "thank you" usually does the job.

Other Helpful Tips to Use During the Prioritization Process

As students are engaged in a full-throttle discussion about which questions to make their priority ones, they may revert to familiar student behavior and call you over to answer a question, clarify or simply to settle the matter with a voice of authority. It's

TABLE 6.1

Tips for prioritizing questions

Students may . . .	Teacher's role
At first, focus on trying to figure out what the teacher wants, and may try to directly draw the teacher into the prioritization process.	Refrain from being pulled into their prioritization discussion or engaging in a back and forth with students.
Ask teacher about how to choose	Respond to any questions with a reminder to the class as a whole about the criteria the teacher set for selecting the priority questions.
Want teachers to give their opinions, to weigh in and clarify "Is this what you mean by a priority question?" or "What is an example of a question we should choose?"	Do not judge, positively or negatively, any questions being considered by the students as priority questions as they are discussing them
Want models of a priority question	*Do not* model a prioritization process or give suggestions about possible priority questions. Modeling will push students to prioritizing questions in the same direction as your example.
Want confirmation that they are on right track	Do not respond positively or negatively to student questions. Teachers should withhold judgment.
Have too few questions	Just make sure students have enough questions to complete this step. Students should have a minimum of five to six questions in their list in order to prioritize.
Be unable to agree on which three questions	As a last resort change the strategy and instruct students to choose three questions individually or for each student to choose her/his most important question.
Want to choose more than three questions	Encourage students to choose three. It is not a big problem if they choose four questions. They just have to explain why they could not let go of the fourth question.

a trap. You'll need to stay keenly aware that your role during the process should be to help the students learn how to manage the process for themselves.

Table 6.1 shows some of the practices that are good to keep in mind while the process is going on.

CONCLUSION

Your students have now completed a very challenging and stimulating section of the QFT. They engaged deeply in thinking about the value and relative importance of all the questions they asked. They are stimulated by what they have figured out and by the similarities and differences between their questions and those they hear from other groups. They are eager to move on to the next steps: *How are we going to use these questions?* That's exactly where we are going in the next chapter.

Key Points

- The ability to prioritize is an essential learning skill as well as life skill.
- Students prioritize their questions based on criteria the teacher establishes.
- Students will learn from each other as they discuss and debate which questions should be the priority ones.
- Teachers should monitor group work, but should be careful not to model or give too much direction for the selection of the priority questions.
- To reinforce their ability to prioritize, students need to provide a rationale for why they chose their priority questions.

CHAPTER 7

Next Steps

"What Do We Do with All These Questions?"

*"The most useful thing I learned from this class was
to learn to ask questions to get better understanding."*

THE STUDENTS AND TEACHERS IN PREVIOUS CHAPTERS have played a game of intellectual ping-pong. It began with the teacher's design of a Question Focus, and then progressed by going back and forth: the teacher asking students to think about the Rules for Producing Questions, students producing questions; the teacher introducing closed- and open-ended questions, the students thinking about those kinds of questions, then changing their questions; the teacher setting ground rules for prioritization, the students engaging in convergent thinking to prioritize their questions. The back and forth concludes with the students' identifying priority questions and explaining the rationale behind their selections.

It could be time to stop. The students have certainly earned a break. They have, after all, gone from inchoate and uninformed notions about a general topic—the original QFocus—through a rigorous winnowing process until they have reached, by consensus or vote, the three final priority questions. That's quite an achievement on its own. This deliberative process alone would serve as a model of collaborative learning and as a resource for more informed decision making.

It could end here—except that the priority questions serve to jump-start, improve and accelerate their learning, not end it. Now is the time to *use* the questions and move on to the next steps.

MANY OPTIONS FOR USING THE QUESTIONS

The Question Formulation Technique offers the teacher an unfiltered opportunity to see, hear, and think about the questions on a student's mind. And it offers students a chance to hear the questions that fellow students have on their minds. Once aired and written down, the questions can be productively used in many different classroom and school situations. Some teachers and students get so comfortable using the QFT that it just becomes part of their regular classroom practice.

For example, a teacher, might use the QFT to start off a class with a *do-now*—having students use the Rules for Producing Questions to generate questions; or students can generate questions at the end of class (this is quite different from the clicker system being used in some college classrooms to see what information was absorbed by students in a lecture). Students might also come up with questions to use as guides for reading or thinking about a new assignment, subject, or topic before being formally introduced to it. They might create questions to shape their own homework assignments or prepare for tests. A teacher might want students to ask questions as part of a mid-unit assessment to see what kinds of questions students are asking and what are they not asking. This provides valuable insight into what the students understood from earlier work and what they still need to learn in upcoming classes.

Because students learn more effectively and seem to retain information more efficiently if they have already asked their own questions, the QFT is a relevant tool that can be used for many purposes. A school might also use the QFT as part of an orientation process for entering students, or as part of an exercise to help transfer students understand the rules, expectations, and benchmarks that might be different from what they have experienced in other schools

The box "Sample Uses of Student Questions" shows just a few of the many ways questions generated by students can be used across all subject areas and grade levels.

EXAMPLES FROM THE CLASSROOM: USE OF QUESTIONS TO BEGIN A PROJECT

The teachers you have met in earlier chapters went on to use their students' questions pretty much as they had planned when they first looked at why and how they would deploy the QFT to further their teaching goals and improve learning outcomes.

The students in Ling-Se Peet's humanities class selected their priority questions to guide a Socratic seminar focused on Julia Alvarez' novel, *In the Time of the Butterflies*. The original QFocus, "Torture can be justified," pushed students to think harder and deeper about the definition, use, and implications of torture. They felt a strong sense of ownership, since their questions would shape the seminar. Even as they entered a learning environment named after a sage who asked all the questions, they as well as Peet were keenly aware that they had just changed the seminar dynamic in a significant way. Students entered the seminar already thinking for themselves—not because of a question the teacher posed to them, but because of the questions they had generated.

Marcy Ostberg's biology class designed experiments related to her original QFocus, "Pollution harms Boston residents." They used their questions to shape and design their experiments as well as to inform and prioritize their research and information-gathering tasks. Marcy observed that the questions allowed the students to go deeper and more quickly into the experiment than she had seen in other classes.

Hayley Dupuy's sixth-graders enthusiastically plowed into projects related to the original QFocus "Plate tectonics affect geography and communities." The students selected the top-priority question they wanted to work on, collaborated with others who shared an interest in that question, and began an in-depth research process to come up with an answer. A month and a half later, they had produced PowerPoint and multimedia presentations that met the rigorous standards their teacher had set. They also proudly presented to their handiwork one evening to an impressed group of parents.

These three teachers used the QFT and the questions generated in the process at or near the beginning of their units to help them achieve their teaching goals. In the rest of this chapter, you will see three additional examples that highlight variations on the use of the QFT and student questions. You will see that students can use their questions continuously or at any time in a unit, up to the very end.

The examples below are drawn from instructors who have become very comfortable with facilitating student questioning. They demonstrate how the questions

---

Sample Uses of Student Questions

Beginning of Unit/Class

- In a do-now activity, students ask questions relevant to previous day's work or upcoming work or any topic to inform class discussion.
- Students generate questions to use as guides for reading or thinking about a new assignment, subject, or topic before being formally introduced to it.
- Students use questions to identify specific topics for research papers, essays, experiments, and projects.
- Teacher uses student questions to assess prior knowledge and identify gaps in information and understanding.
- Teacher uses student questions to shape or refine lesson plans for the next day or entire unit.
- Student questions guide Socratic seminar content.
- Teacher posts student questions for them to see as unit progresses.

Midunit or Middle of Class

- Students generate questions to shape their own homework assignments.
- Questions provide examples for teachers to review in prep for next stage of unit.
- Students use questions to prepare for tests.

---

can be woven in to the flow of both student learning and key lessons they want to impart to their students in more traditional ways:

1. **Thinking as mathematicians:** Student questions in a math class continuously push the boundaries of their learning and prepare the ground for understanding more deeply the relevance of traditional problem-solving methods.
2. **Student questions drive the research agenda:** Students in a multidisciplinary project use their questions in research and project-based learning to learn and accomplish more than they or their teachers thought possible

- Questions help teacher assess what kinds of issues students are addressing and what they are not and what students are and are not understanding or learning.

- Teacher references student questions from beginning of unit to show how they are being answered through student work.

- Questions can guide moot court exercises in which students in the role of judges prepare questions to ask of lawyers and students as lawyers try to predict questions they will hear from opposing counsel and judge.[1]

- Students prepare questions for job exploration.

End of Unit/Class

- In a do-now activity at end of class, students ask questions relevant to the class just concluded or next day's work or upcoming work or any topic.

- Student questions help them prepare final reports, PowerPoint presentations, and write papers.

- Students use questions to prepare for interviewing outside experts.

- Questions aid in final assessment and review of student learning.

- Students and teacher set new research agenda for the next unit.

- Teacher references student questions from beginning of unit to show how they have been answered through student work and works with students to identify questions that still need answer.

3. **Student questions release the "unlock" button:** When faced with a difficult writing assignment, a student's questions serve as the catalyst for figuring things out and overcoming previously insurmountable obstacles.

CASE STUDY: "THINKING AS MATHEMATICIANS"

Teacher: Jimmy Frickey, Eagle Rock School and Professional Development Center, Colorado

Subject: Mathematics
Class size: Twenty-five students
QFocus: Different math problems
Purpose in using QFT: Asking questions as mathematicians

Jimmy Frickey's students at the Eagle Rock School and Professional Development Center in Colorado were about to be part of an ambitious experiment in the use of their own questions. They had all arrived at the small, full-scholarship boarding school with a similar profile: they had not experienced much success in traditional academic programs and did not expect to graduate from high school. They entered Frickey's math class conditioned to think that their job was to finish a problem set, turn in the answers, and wait to get the next set from the teacher. Frickey wanted them to shift from thinking about turning in answers to turning answers into questions. This was no small task—by changing the dynamics of the traditional student-teacher relationship, he was about to challenge this group of students who had not done well before in math to begin "thinking like mathematicians."

Frickey started them off by giving them a relatively simple problem to solve, one that he was confident most of them could either solve or at least understand the solution. After they took some time to work on it, he asked for a volunteer to present a solution and explain why it was correct. There was nothing out of the ordinary up to this point. But then Frickey challenged them to take the answer they had just come up with and generate new questions about it. The answer to the previous question had now become a Question Focus.

As the students generated questions, Frickey, serving as scribe, wrote them on the board. Each student then chose one question to work on further. When they finished working on that math question, they again presented their solutions and repeated the process.

Frickey continued this process through the first week of the course. He then worked with the students to map all their questions, showing them just how many they had produced in a relatively short time. The students could see the starting question in a bubble at the center of the map. Arrows emanated outward to smaller bubbles, where the new questions would be placed. Those smaller bubbles would also include a brief part of the answer to those questions.

Students soon got used to this flow; answering a question and generating new questions, answering those, sharing their work with the whole class, and then selecting an answer as a new QFocus for generating even more questions. The process helped them take apart and drill down deep inside of a math problem from different perspectives. In one session, they were grappling with a classic mathematical word problem, the *broken-egg problem*, which pushes deeper thinking about integers. It goes like this:

A farmer is taking her eggs to the market when her cart hits a pothole. The cart tips over, and every egg is broken. So she goes to her insurance agent, who asks her how many eggs she had. She says she doesn't know, but she remembers something from various ways she tried packing the eggs. When she put the eggs in groups of two, three, four, five, and six, there was one egg left over, but when she put them in groups of seven they ended up in complete groups with no eggs left over.

What can the farmer figure from this information about the number of eggs she had? Is there more than one answer?

Several students spent some time asking about different ways to divide a number. One student asked, "What happens if it groups evenly with six eggs [meaning divisible by six]?" while another student worked on the complications that might ensue from different ways of grouping the eggs. Another student wanted to know: "What happens for seven eggs?" Then, one student, focusing on a bigger question, asked: "What are the divisibility rules?" This girl, Frickey noted, remembered that there are ways to tell when a number is divisible by certain numbers, but didn't remember the rule. However, hearing the series of previous questions helped her gain a new appreciation for rules and realize that it would be easier to solve these word problems if she could consistently employ the divisibility rules.

Frickey would use these student-generated questions or choose appropriate times to provide a more traditional lesson about *mathematical questions*—the types of questions mathematicians ask. He tapped into pedagogical resources for problem-posing strategies and demonstrated, for example, how mathematicians change their questions by altering or restricting or relaxing a feature of the problem as they try to solve it.

His lessons helped stretch and expand the students' understanding. They became more flexible thinkers and better problem solvers. At one point, Frickey reports, their questions were informed by one of his lessons about the use of tables to organize information "in the hopes of recognizing a pattern. The table allowed the group to make the conjecture that broken-egg problems that end with a prime number can be solved, and others cannot. This conjecture is awfully close to a famous mathematical theorem, the Chinese Remainder Theorem." They were now, just as he had hoped, "thinking like mathematicians."

The course continued for five weeks, and Frickey was regularly impressed by the energy in the class that came from giving the students the power to ask their own questions: "Students tended to choose problem variations that were of interest to them, and the combination of the choice and interest . . . dramatically increased their commitment to and engagement in their work for the course . . . This also turned out to be a powerful differentiated learning practice." He was also struck about how effective the process was as a differentiation strategy, noting, "Confident students tended to ask and choose more challenging problems, while less confident students tended to ask and choose simple variations of the starting problem. Still, all solutions added to the class's collective knowledge of this class of problem."

There was indeed a lot of energy in his classroom. It was not the first time Frickey had seen this phenomenon; he had "occasionally been able to create some pretty engaging lessons using various techniques." Getting students to ask their own questions, however, was different. It became a way of working, a methodology that energized his students regularly, as opposed to a one-time special lesson.

He observed this up close, but was surprised and delighted to hear confirmation of engaged and energized students from fellow teachers. They told him that they had heard his students continuing the discussion of the specific math problems and what they learned in class while on a field trip as well as at meal times. When students got this energized by asking their own questions, Jimmy felt that his responsibilities as a teacher changed: "My job went from trying to engage students and bring out their energy to instead having to manage their energy, even interrupt them working on a problem to [get them to] stop and listen to someone else. The change for me was undeniable."

CASE STUDY: STUDENT QUESTIONS DRIVE THE RESEARCH AGENDA

Teachers: Sara Fass, Aaron Stone, and Rachel Jean-Marie, Boston Day and Evening Academy (BDEA)

Subject: Science, mathematics, and humanities
Class size: Twenty students
QFocus: *Cigarette smoking*
Purpose in using QFT: Research and projects

A science teacher, a math teacher and a humanities teacher enter a classroom. It's not the opening to a joke but rather a description of an impressive collaborative effort to teach a unit on the health effects of smoking at BDEA. The three teachers, Sara Fass, Aaron Stone, and Rachel Jean-Marie, decided to use the QFT to jump-start and guide the unit. They wanted students to identify priority questions that would shape their research and help them generate a range of projects and products.

They used a very barebones QFocus:

Cigarette smoking.

The students got started. Fass reported that they soon "came up with more questions than I've ever seen a group of students come up with before." They pushed and prodded each other in different directions:

- Why are cigarettes harmful?
- What is in a cigarette?
- Why sell cigarettes if they are deadly?
- Why do cigarettes have so many chemicals?
- Who invented cigarettes?
- Why is that 'warning label' on the cigarette box?
- What are different ways of quitting?
- What will it take for stores to stop selling cigarettes?
- Is there a type of NA class for people who smoke?
- Do you think that this world would be without cigarettes one day?
- Why are cigarettes legal?
- What do you think can be done to prevent people from smoking?

Fass's pleasant surprise at how many questions the students generated echoes the response of many other teachers who use the QFT. She was very satisfied with the *quantity* of the questions. But what did she make of the *quality* of the questions?

Some, in her opinion, were better than others, but she let the students prioritize the questions on their own. When they got through their prioritization process, they chose the following question to guide their research: "Why is that warning label on the cigarette box?"

Fass was surprised again, but not so pleasantly this time. She was, in fact, "kind of annoyed when they decided that would be their top priority question." She just did not see why the students chose that one, "considering [that] some of the other questions that they brainstormed seemed deeper." She thought "one of the deeper questions was 'Why are cigarettes legal?'" which she perceived as "a really juicy question." Despite her misgivings, she and the other teachers felt it was important to allow the students to work, at least at the outset, on their chosen question.

She was in for another surprise: she had never seen the students more motivated and engaged in the learning process. They looked at the specific ingredients of cigarettes and gathered information about why some of the chemicals are added. They examined the science of addiction to nicotine and explored different ways to quit smoking. They interviewed smokers about why they had started smoking, continued to smoke, or quit smoking and how. They even attended a "Kick Butts Day!" at the State House and heard from youth antismoking activists and state officials.

Fass had wanted the group's research to focus on the impact of smoking on their health. They wound up looking at that and much more. The class had uncovered multiple layers of complexity related to the issue of cigarette smoking. They had studied the chemistry of the cigarette and the science of addiction and the challenges of behavioral and physical change, and had also examined statistics illustrating personal and societal implications of cigarette-related illnesses. They also examined legal and public policy matters related to smoking—and took action and created their own response to the problem. By the end of their research, the students had a deeper and more thorough understanding of the effects of smoking and demonstrated their knowledge in various ways. They used statistics they had uncovered to design antismoking t-shirts and create poster boards that drew attention to the implications of cigarette smoking for society in general.

They had worked hard and learned a lot, and it all began with and was guided by their questions. Fass was struck by "how much could be done with one QFocus." She also understood the significance of the shift in how the research agenda was established. She and her fellow teachers had created and set the overall direction of the unit, but the students had driven the research: "Even if I had given them an assignment 'Study the effects described by the warning,' they would have just been responding once again to a teacher's request. Instead, they felt real ownership of this and produced amazing work showing just how much can be learned from looking closely at that warning label. At the end, they started looking at warning labels from other countries and asking, 'Why is the warning label in the U.S. so weak?'"

The students concluded the assignment, and like Jimmy Frickey's math class, transformed their answers into a new question and a new research agenda. But they also did something else. At the end of all their exploring, they looked again at their original research question about the warning labels on the cigarette boxes, and, informed by their research and action, created their own alternative warning labels:

- It's a killa!!!
- Don't smoke: Doctor's Orders!
- Caution: Smoke at your own risk
- Just Don't Do It (with Nike logo upside down)
- Got cigarettes? Got cancer!
- Smoking = death
- Deadly
- Suicide can be fast or slow (cigarettes)

STUDENT QUESTIONS RELEASE THE "UNLOCK BUTTON"

The students at Eagle Rock School and the students at the Boston Day and Evening Academy responded enthusiastically and with great intellectual energy to the open but rigorous process of the QFT. They fed off each other as they asked questions and learned from each other's line of inquiry. Their work as a class or in small groups created what new-media scholar Clay Shirky describes as a kind of "cognitive surplus" where they wind up having access to more knowledge than they could have obtained on their own.[2]

But what happens if you are working with an individual student who gets stuck and can't come up with many or even any questions? Can you get students working on their own to generate their own questions?

Marcy Ostberg has found that she can use the QFT in her science classes at the Boston Day and Evening Academy as a way to get individual students "unstuck" when they do not seem to get key points she wants them to understand. But, she says, when they start asking questions, "[it] seems to unlock something for them."

Ostberg is on to something with that observation. First, it is important to use the QFT as an informal resource to invite students to try to think of their own questions. They have generally not done that in their schooling, so just the granting of the license to ask can often be powerful enough to get them to ask questions that otherwise would never have been asked. Second, when they try to come up with questions, their minds are being pushed and stretched to think in a different way. The results might not show up immediately or the first time they do it but if they persevere and use the QFT consistently on their own, they will steadily develop their own "question-asking" muscle.

And once they start asking questions, they will hear questions they have not thought of before, think about a problem from a different angle, and will, as Ostberg put it, "unlock something." It's an experience we all have had at one point or another. Just asking or hearing a question phrased a certain way produces an almost palpable feeling of discovery and new understanding. Questions, more than any other utterance, have a particularly powerful influence: they produce the "lightbulb" effect. It is no surprise, then that even the greatest thinkers spend their days trying to figure out what questions to ask and how to turn on that one lightbulb that will shed light on where they need to go in their investigations.

How does a question turn on the lightbulb? How does the asking of the question unlock or activate the brain so that we can see exactly what we had been missing? Perhaps at some point in the near future, it will be possible to study exactly which part of the brain becomes active or is more developed when there is a strong question-asking ability. We would like to see more research on the brain activity related to asking questions by cognitive psychologists and neuroscientists.

In the meantime, we have more than enough evidence of those palpable moments of insight and greater clarity that have been reported by teachers using the QFT in their classrooms. The immediate benefit they observe is related to content—the student acquires a new or deeper understanding of the course or lesson material. The sustained, long-term benefit relates to developing a transferable skill and a change in how the student perceives himself or herself. The students realize, plain and simple, that they now have an ability to think and problem solve on their own, abilities they didn't know they had in them.

Case Study: A Volunteer Helps a Student Unlock His Questions to Write a Speech

The national community service organization City Year is engaged in a multicity dropout-prevention effort. A cohort of idealistic seventeen- to twenty-four-year-old corps members are placed in schools to support teachers by working with at-risk students. In one small New Hampshire community, Paul Riley, a City Year corps member serving as a tutor, found a way to use the QFT to good effect when working with a particularly discouraged and frustrated seventh grade student.

The teacher had given the class an assignment that looked promising. She was trying to engage them in setting their own learning agenda by requesting that they choose an article to read, ask a question about the article, and then write a speech to answer that question. It was an assignment rich in reading, writing, and communications potential. This teacher, however, did not know about the QFT and did not have a method in place to help students generate even the one question they would answer in their speech.

Riley found his charge, Kevin, particularly unhappy with the task. He had no idea how to begin and he had zero interest in doing it. He didn't get what it meant for him to come up with a question, and as Riley observed, Kevin "[never] liked writing assignments, and often only writes a few sentences when much longer paragraphs are required."

Eventually, pressed by an impending deadline, Kevin decided on an article. He knew young men and women in his community who were serving in Iraq, and this helped interest him in learning more about what was happening there. He had found an article about the role of Blackwater, the private security company, and its role in the deaths of seventeen Iraqi civilians.[3] He was willing to read the article, he told Riley, but said he could "only write two sentences on it."

Student and tutor found themselves stuck in what was by now a very familiar dead-end for both of them. Kevin said he couldn't write anything and Riley, was trying, without putting words in his mouth, to get him to write more. It did not look promising.

Riley, however, decided to creatively use one part of the QFT to find a way out of the impasse and onto a more productive path. He created, on the spot, different

QFocus statements to help Kevin press the "unlock button" and free his mind to start seeing how much he could ask and how much more there was to write about.

For example, Riley, posed the article's title, "F.B.I. Says Guards Killed 14 Iraqis Without Cause," as a QFocus and requested that Kevin generate questions. Kevin asked: "Why did they do it?" He was sure that question alone was sufficient for writing the speech. He wrote it down and considered himself done.

But Riley pushed him to ask some more questions. Kevin hesitated and then asked: "Who is Blackwater?" Riley thought to himself: "Well, we both know the answer to that because we just read the article about them that also described them as a military company." But then he turned that fact into a new QFocus: "Blackwater is a military company working in Iraq."

This repositioning of information into a QFocus triggered a more interested look on Kevin's face. Riley pushed onward and encouraged Kevin to think about questions he could ask about this statement. Kevin thought for a bit and then asked: "Why is a military company in Iraq?"

This was an important moment for Kevin. He had broken through and asked a question that pushed him in a different direction, moving from a narrow focus on Blackwater to a broader focus on the role of something called a military company in the context of the U.S. Armed Forces role in Iraq. He went on to ask a few more questions, but eventually settled on this one as the focus for his speech. He wound up writing more than he had ever written before, surprising himself as well as his teacher.

In this one-to-one relationship, Riley had nimbly created new QFocus statements on the fly to get his student to generate more questions. It was a riff on using the Rules for Producing Questions—in this case, choosing to stimulate Kevin with a new QFocus each time he was about to give up. "The process of having to come up with his own questions," Riley noted, moved a "student who is usually apathetic" to "take control of his own paper."

This is no small accomplishment, as any teacher who has gotten "the look" of "I'm done and I've got nothing more to say" can testify. Kevin's classroom teacher had given an interesting assignment, designed to actually try to promote student ownership, but he perceived it as an overwhelming and impossible task. He might, he conceded, manage to find an article to read and read it, but the notion of coming up with his own question to answer in a written speech was beyond what he thought could ever do.

Kevin, who was usually "apathetic," was ready to call it quits. Thanks to Paul Riley, who creatively offered him opportunities to ask questions, he generated new ones, unlocked his own potential, and wrote and delivered a speech.

CONCLUSION

If the students described in this chapter are to fully see the significance of what just happened, if they are to internalize what they accomplished and what it means for them in the future, the work cannot end here. They need to go one more step. They need the opportunity to name for themselves what they have learned, why it is valuable, and how they can continue to use the process of creating questions beyond this one assignment.

Students can do this and articulate their perspective on genuine learning in thoughtful, deep, and original ways. Giving them the chance to reflect, articulate, and record the implications of what they just did is giving them another too rare, but invaluable gift, and it increases the chances that the learning and the new skill will stay with them.

The next chapter lays out a simple process to facilitate student reflection that will benefit your students and provide you and your students with hard evidence of the significance of what you both just accomplished.

Key Points

- Student questions can be used for multiple purposes.
- Student questions can be used by the students themselves, as part of group or class projects, by the teachers and by students and teachers working together.

CHAPTER 8

Students Reflect on Their Learning

Cognition, Affect, and Behavior

*"When I ask questions, it helps me by knowing what
I am studying through my own perspective. It allows me
to question myself as well as the subject."*

*"I think asking your own questions is important
because when you ask questions and answer them
yourself its like learning by yourself."*

THE PROCESS IS DONE . . . or maybe not quite yet.

Students have produced their own questions. They have improved their questions as they learned how to change closed and open-ended questions. Using criteria provided by the teacher, they have thought strategically about their questions, assessed and compared their relative value, and then selected three priority questions. They are now ready to use their questions for whatever you have designated as the next steps: for projects, as a guide for further reading, to write a paper, or just to get them thinking before introducing a new topic.

There's one more step that is remarkably revealing and profoundly important for both students and teachers—*reflection*. Students are asked to reflect on the whole process, and, as a result, they deepen their learning, develop greater confidence for moving forward and applying their newly developed skill, and reveal to their teachers a new depth of understanding that may not have previously been detected.

REINFORCING LEARNING, STRENGTHENING METACOGNITION, ENSURING CONTINUED APPLICATION

When students are asked to reflect on the process they just experienced, they are looking back at what has come before and thinking about it from their current perspective. They are naming what has (and has not) been understood. They are identifying what they have learned and how it affects their thinking and feeling now. And they get the chance to name what it felt like going through the experience and what they can do in the future with what they just learned. That's a lot more thinking.

It is tempting, in the rush to get on to the next steps, to skip reflection. But after your students have learned how to produce, improve, and prioritize their questions, the act of reflection on what they learned will deepen their metacognitive skills—and that is essential for insuring they will be able to use again and again the question-formulation skill and thinking abilities they just practiced. If this step is skipped, there is a danger that the question formulation process will be one more classroom exercise whose importance teachers recognize, but that the students follow only because the teachers require it. Reflection gives students the opportunity to name for themselves what they are learning, and when they do that, they own the skills more strongly and deepen their understanding of how they can use what they learned in other situations.

There's an important benefit to reflection for you, as a teacher, as well. First of all, you deserve the chance to hear students name for themselves the value of something you designed and they just did. You brought the innovation into the classroom; you should hear about the impact you just had on your students. Second, you will hear and read (if you ask them to provide written reflections) about which parts of the process took hold in their minds. You will get immediate feedback that can help you see how something that seems so ordinary—for example, just learning about the difference between closed- and open-ended questions—is new and significant for your students. You can also use the reflection process to ask students directly what they learned related to the content and your curricular goals. The reflection process provides you with immediate and relevant feedback on your teaching and their learning.

THE REFLECTION PROCESS

The goal of this step is for students to think about the work they have done in the QFT process. You will need to decide what you want to learn from students and how to organize the reflection activity or activities. A minimum of five minutes will be needed. The process can develop as follows:

1. **Develop the reflection activity:**
   - What do you want to learn from students?
   - What do you want students to think about?

2. **Decide how to facilitiate the reflection activity:** You can use a variety of strategies for students to reflect. Some of the same strategies you already use for students for thinking about their work and reporting will be effective:
   - *Individual reflection:* Students individually spend three minutes answering the reflection questions. They can then share in small groups or with the large group.
   - *Small group reflection with reports to large group:* Small groups discuss the questions and jot down notes to report to large group. Students can choose one speaker to report or volunteers share their thoughts.
   - *Large group reflection:* You pose the reflection questions for students to answer and ask for volunteers to share.

3. **Support students during the reflection process:**
   - Make sure students stay on task while they share in small groups.
   - Encourage all students to share when reflecting in large group.
   - Try to validate all contributions equally as students comment or report.

4. **Create a classroom process/structure for doing the reflection:** There are many ways to do the reflection, and each one brings specific benefits to the process. You should think about what will work best for your classroom. Here are some options:
   - Working in small groups, students discuss reflection questions and report a summary of the discussion to the class as a whole.
   - The teacher leads discussion with the class as a whole.
   - Students write their reflections on their own and then turn them in.
   - Students write their reflections and share them with partners or with small groups or with larger groups before turning them in to the teacher.

DESIGNING THE REFLECTION ACTIVITY

The first part of this process is to design a reflection activity. You will need to decide on what you want to learn from students and how to help them think about the work they've done. You may want to see the reflection process as a way to gather information related to content, comprehension, skill development, and intellectual growth. You can structure the activity to capture multiple perspectives. You'll now be going back to the familiar model of the teacher posing the questions and the students responding to teacher's questions.

As the students think about the work they did and what they learned, they need a chance to name discoveries about what they know (cognitive), how they feel (affective) and what they are able to do (behavioral). Here are some examples of questions that you can use in the reflection process.

Reflection Questions About Cognitive Changes

The following questions address the amount and kind of knowledge that the QFT brought to the students.

What did you learn? This is a very open-ended question that allows students to choose any step in the process that was particularly relevant to them. Some students will focus on the process, others will focus on content or even on the changes on student-teacher relationship during the process, for example:

- "I learned how to ask questions. I also learned how to improve the questions I ask."
- "I learned that open questions are good for essential question and closed are good for lab experiments."

Why is learning to ask your own questions important for learning? This question is more specific and looks at the value of the questions and the value of asking them for learning:

- "This helps us develop certain skills."
- "This helps our brain work."
- "Learning how to ask questions helps us get information faster. Also it helps us get straight to the point."

What did you learn about [the content] that we are studying? You can frame the reflection questions to get at content. For example, Laurie Gaughran, the history teacher we met in the introduction, had her students at Humanities Prep compare the 1863 race riots in New York with the 1993 race riots in Los Angeles. She asked two questions: "What have you learned from the practice of asking questions?" and "How has it influenced your learning about these two riots?" These are responses from two of her students:

- "I learned that asking questions is such a simple thing but, at the same time, can open up towards so much opportunity to learn. Also inquiring so frequently about the two riots allows me to gain perspective on them that the people during the riots wouldn't have been able to have. This is from the benefit of being an outside evaluator, almost two decades in the future."
- "I have learned that asking questions helps us receive a deeper understanding of a topic. We're not just randomly talking about a topic, we are answering questions that we can answer for each other. It helps us go in depth about a topic and it has raised unknown answers for me about questions I had about the riot. We didn't just learn and compare the riots. We learned how each occurred, what happened, important people and why it happened."

How did you learn it?   This reflection question looks at the process itself and allows students an opportunity to think about the different steps. It also helps students think about how they worked in collaboration with each other:

- "We got to rewrite questions."
- "We also got to change the question to try to get more info. I also liked how we ask questions without being questioned."
- "We all worked together."
- "We heard questions from others that were different from ours. That helped us to think about new questions too."

Reflection Questions About the Affective Impact

The following questions can elicit reflections on students' personal responses to the process, opening up another whole area of reflection:

How do you feel now about asking questions?   This question can come as a surprise to students. In Ling-Se Peet's ninth-grade summer school class, some of the students were flummoxed:

- "I don't really know, Miss, how I feel."

Others said:

- "I feel smart."
- "I feel like I'm getting good at this questions thing."

Students in other classrooms talk about how much they like working in small groups, or being able to do the thinking for themselves, without the teacher telling them what to think."

- "It makes me feel like I can figure things out for myself."

What did you like about the work you did? This question gets to the affective aspect of the QFT. It gives students an opportunity to think about and name what they liked and how they felt when using the process. Responses included:

- "I like that it lets you focus on a specific topic. This is a great way to form project ideas, also because I personally ended up asking questions that I never would have thought of before. I also think it's fun to be allowed to spout out random questions."
- "I liked it because the process didn't exclude any questions. This made it so anybody could ask whatever they wanted. This was an interesting process."

Reflection Questions on Possible Behavioral Changes

The third type of question is directed at uncovering how the QFT has affected student behavior. It asks what students will do differently as a result of learning to ask their own questions.

How can you use what you learned about asking questions? A student in a class using a Facing History and Ourselves curriculum for seventh graders said: "I will use it in life and also in my other classes." A summer school student in Boston answered: "I learned that you can turn a statement into a question and you can use that in real life." And another student responded, "You can use the skill of asking questions for later in life. You know how to solve problems."

Two students in Hayley Dupuy's middle school class thought about how they could apply what they were learning to other assignments and in other classes:

- "I could use that process again when brainstorming for almost any project. It would work best when coming up with how to turn a big topic into a smaller, more specific one."
- "I could use that process on my own while writing. I could ask myself questions about my plot and characters and decide on a story."

These are just examples of reflection questions you can pose to your students. You may want to develop others that help your students name what they learned and help you learn more from them about where they are at the end of the process and how it is different from where they were before you used the QFT. It is an essential step that helps students internalize all they have done.

TROUBLESHOOTING REFLECTING

You might encounter some challenges while helping students reflect. Below are some tips on how to troubleshoot this part of the process:

- **There is no time left for reflection in the class period:** Give the reflection as an assignment. Facilitate the reflection on a different day. It is very important for the internalization of the skill to not skip this step of the process.
- **Some students tell you that they have not learned anything:** This should not be a concern. There will be a range of responses to the QFT experience. Allow the students to react honestly. Sometimes you will find students who don't see an immediate value but realize later on that what they learned can be useful in many situations. Acknowledge their contribution. Encourage them to keep in mind the steps they went through.
- **Getting the quiet student to reflect and share:** Sharing will help quiet students gain confidence. To help them you might ask them to do some thinking individually before sharing. For example, ask them to jot down some thoughts about the reflection question and then share with a partner or in their small group.

You can also ask students to take turns reporting or to report for each other. Make sure to validate all contributions equally.

- **Reporting and group dynamics:** The reporting step in the reflection allows students to learn from each other and to see how they approached the topic from different perspectives. It is important that all students share. Help students listen to other groups' reports by asking them to pay attention to what is similar or different from what they discussed. You can follow up by asking for their observations on the similarities and differences.

CONCLUSION

Your students have now completed the entire process of the Question Formulation Technique. When you introduce them to the process for the first time, they may be intellectually spent by the time they get to the end. If, however, they are more experienced in using the QFT, you will soon see how quickly they move through the process, how comfortable they get with it, and how, by the end, they may have more energy than they had at the beginning.

Your commitment to facilitating the process several times is very important. Some classes will get in the flow the very first time and some may require a couple more opportunities. The first time you use it, may even remind you of your first time in the classroom, except that you'll climb this learning curve so quickly that you will be an expert by your third time using it. In the next chapter, you'll hear a teacher's perspective on the learning curve for using the QFT in the classroom.

Key Points

- Do not skip over the reflection step.
- Set aside a minimum of five to eight minutes for reflection.
- During the reflection process, you return to your role of asking questions and the students return to their roles of responding to your questions.
- Students can reflect individually, in small groups or as a large group.
- Validate students equally when listening to their reports.

CHAPTER 9

A Memo to My Fellow Teachers

What I've Learned from Using the QFT

"I learned that asking questions can be just as important as a teacher asking questions."

BELOW IS A MEMO *addressing some of the pitfalls, challenges, and rewards teachers encounter when using the Question Formulation Technique in their classrooms. It is written in the voice of one teacher, but actually pulls together advice from a number of teachers who have been sharing their new expertise in the use of the QFT in various formats: informal conversations with colleagues, documentation of student work, faculty discussions, sharing of teaching materials and ideas, and professional development workshops they offered in their own schools.*

TO: My Fellow Teachers
RE: The shift in my teaching when I teach my students to formulate their own questions

As you know, I have started to use a simple strategy, called the Question Formulation Technique, in my classroom to build my students' question formulation skills. Here's the essence of what I've learned by using it:

- What seems difficult is possible—teaching students to ask their own questions.
- What seems simple isn't simplistic—using just a few steps to teach them the skill.

- What isn't simple can be done—making students more independent learners by developing the skill to ask their own questions.
- It makes my job easier and helps my students more than I could have imagined.
- And when it's done, it's worth it—more than I ever dreamed it would be.

The "difficult" you already know: the idea that students will ask their own questions. You've already seen the questions my students have produced, what we've done with their questions, and what they themselves have said about how much they like doing it and how much they've learned. And some of you have told me about my students who are now asking questions in *your* class for the first time ever. That is exciting to hear.

The one-page card, "The RQI Question Formulation Technique" appendix, lays out the entire Question Formulation Technique. It all looks pretty simple, no long training manuals to absorb, no new content to review. Maybe the only new word there is *Question Focus*, which is really just a "prompt" in our language, but stated differently to make sure that we and our students remember they're the ones coming up with the questions, not responding to our question.

It might even seem so obvious as to be simplistic. But it's not. There is that one small change that makes all the difference; from me thinking up the questions and asking questions of my students to getting my students to *generate their own questions*. That is basically the whole point.

ONE BIG CHANGE: STUDENTS ARE THE ONES ASKING QUESTIONS

Getting the students to ask their own questions may be the whole point, but it's not something that comes naturally.

I have seen how much my students struggle to ask a question when they're bogged down. That's why I've always used questions to help get them unstuck. I find that I can generally lead them through a process, probing with my questions, to help them get to a better place. But I also saw that too often they became dependent on me to lead them through a similar process as soon as we moved on to another subject or assignment. Now I realize I was doing a lot of the heavy lifting for them when I was figuring out which questions would get them out of the mire.

I had to work at not asking questions, even to help my students. That's hard. Harder than I thought it might be.

You know how, if you pick up a pen with your dominant hand and start writing, you don't stop to think about it. Of course, you may pause to think about what you are writing—generally a good practice—but you don't think about the mechanics of writing and you certainly are not thinking about the way the pen is positioned gently but securely between your thumb and other fingers. There's absolutely nothing strange about it. It goes without notice.

But all that changes if you temporarily disable your dominant hand. Break a finger, sprain your wrist—and all of a sudden, you may need to do everything with your weak hand. Now it's absolutely impossible to avoid thinking about all those things. You have pain from the injury in your dominant hand, and you discover that having to use your weak one for simple tasks is an altogether different kind of pain. I know it doesn't sound enticing, but that's kind of the pain, or at least discomfort, you feel when you have to *refrain from using questions as you prompt students to think in a different way.*

The students also feel your pain, and their own as well, because you're pushing them to do something they're not accustomed to doing either. And you'll need to stand strong on this and push, cajole, and require your students to produce their own questions. There is something going on in their heads when they're pushing hard to come up with their own questions. It's as if they've got this weak, unused "question-asking muscle" that they're trying to use. Give them some time, give them some practice, and watch that muscle grow. I certainly know that when I began developing my own essential questions to guide a discussion or the curriculum for the whole year, I had to do a lot of thinking. I was able to do this only because I had to undergo the process of figuring out a powerful, all-encompassing question. But, now, I'm wondering: how do I develop this ability in my students? It is not about teaching students all about questions, but rather learning how to jump-start the question formulation process so they start working that muscle themselves. Once they are able to do it, we can build on that in many directions.

Well, that's the challenge about the one big change, but it's not the whole story. There are more challenges to using this QFT than meet the eye.

CHANGE BEGINS WITH THE QFOCUS!

Take, for example, the design of the Question Focus. There is some work to be done in learning how to create an effective one, but you will pick that up pretty quickly.

There are some criteria for what makes a good one (I can share that with you), and, just like figuring out a prompt, you will learn to do it. Initially some of your QFocus statements might not work just right, but you will learn through trial and error what works best.

Do Not Give Examples!

Then, there's this small matter of how I teach. I'm accustomed to giving lots of examples to help explain or clarify an assignment. And the students are always asking me for examples. If I don't volunteer one the second they seem confused, they'll pipe up and say—and here's one question they do ask regularly—"Can you give us an example?"

Now, I have to remember *not* to give an example. There's a clear set of *Rules for Producing Questions* that really do get my students thinking in many different directions. They're doing divergent thinking like I've never seen before. But the minute I give them an example, the game's up and they'll conclude, "Oh, that's what the teacher is looking for." And that, for them, is what they believe the game is all about. So that's one of the things we're up against that when we use the QFT.

The first time I used the process, I didn't even realize that I was giving examples, but I did, even if it was in the form of a question. It hit me when I heard the groups report; one of the students got really excited and raised his hand and said, "Did you notice that every group started off with the same question?" I quietly said, "That's probably because they heard me suggest that one to your group when you all asked for help."

That example just shows you how students are waiting to follow our lead. So here are a few things to keep in mind when using the QFT:

- Don't be too quick to help when students are slow to start asking questions.
- Don't ever suggest a question
- Don't give an example of what you're thinking about.

Manage the Groups by Monitoring.

So, if I'm not helping, if I'm not modeling, if I'm not asking my class good questions, and I'm not giving examples—all of which I thought was what I was paid to do—what am I doing all the time my students are working in their small groups?

Well, I'm not checking e-mail, that's for sure. There's a fair amount of small-group management to do. Most of it consists of monitoring the groups at work and ensuring they stay on task. To do that, I basically just have to maintain a kind of "zone of proximity" when I spot some troubles, or maybe I can remind them of my original directions for that particular step.[1] To help keep the groups on task, I might also let them know how much time they have to complete each one of the steps. I've also seen how they'll digress at times—you know the wild range of things they'll start talking about—and that doesn't seem to really keep them from the task. If the digression goes on for too long, I'll get them back to the step, but going off a little sometimes helps them manage their own restlessness. And a sense of accountability kicks in when they realize they're going to have to report to the rest of the groups, so they get back to business with maybe only a slight nudge in that direction from me.

REMIND STUDENTS OF THE RULES!

One of the most challenging parts for me is when my students are first producing their questions. They need to constantly be reminded of the Rules for Producing Questions. The rules are simple but they go against all that's familiar to them—discussing, judging, making statements, etc., about questions as they come up. The rules make it much easier to manage the small groups. When they stop to do anything but ask questions, all you have to do is remind them of the rules. It's not too difficult, but you need to be alert to which groups are not following them and make sure not to get pulled into a discussion with any one of the groups.

So that's one thing you'll do a lot: remind students to follow the rules. It turns out to be a pretty good classroom management technique as well—I know that's not the original purpose, but it works to keep them on task and engaged and to help them self-regulate.

MAKE REFLECTION PART OF THE PROCESS.

There's another thing you'll have to push them to do at various points: *think about their thinking and talk about it.* They are definitely *not* used to doing that, but I can see them beginning to really enjoy it. To get the full benefit of the process, they need to actually think about what they are learning and how they learned it. It definitely makes my day because I can really see what's happening for them. I wouldn't necessarily know how much they are taking in or how they felt about learning to ask their own questions unless I asked them the reflection questions built into the QFT. Most of all, when they get to name what they learned and how—and they see that they did it on their own—you can see their confidence growing. I think the closest I've ever come to this before is when I've asked a few questions of my students at the end of a unit, or maybe only at the end of the year, about what they learned and what they liked the most. I've also done things like KWL but it's just not the same.[2] I have seen that when my students reflect, they can name—in their own words, of course—that they now know how to do divergent thinking, convergent thinking, and metacognitive thinking. And it makes me feel we've really accomplished something. So, not only for their sake, but to give *yourself* a good feeling of what you've done, be sure to ask the reflection questions.

VALIDATE EQUALLY AND WITHOUT JUDGMENT

There's one more challenge I want to mention. This one is really more about style, but it is relevant to getting students to do this thing—asking questions—that seems strange to them. I'm used to trying to pull comments out of them during class discussions. I always encourage them, giving plenty of positive feedback, especially to the students who hardly ever talk. But the key idea in using the QFT is to try to get them to think for themselves unfettered by worries about whether the teacher thinks they've just asked a good question or not. So here's another tough guideline: when the students report their questions, or make comments during any reflection exercise, *try to keep your response neutral.*

This is not easy, but try to refrain from saying "Good question" or "Great question" or "Very good" or the like in response to any particular question, even if a student who never spoke before comes out with a great one. Why would you not give positive reinforcement, especially to that student? Because the other students will start worrying if you don't say the exact same thing to them, and that will stop them from asking more questions. I now use the neutral "Thank you" to acknowledge every student comment. They look at me like it's weird at first, but I've had students tell me they really, really like it because they're usually waiting for the teacher to tell them they did it right or they wind up feeling bad. Staying neutral seems to reinforce the space the QFT gives them to do their own thinking without being judged. This works for all students, including the ones who are already doing well. But I think the space it gives students to think and ask their own questions makes it work especially well for students who have been struggling.

You do want to validate the efforts of all students. But unintentionally placing less value on some of the questions and more on others will show your preferences and might discourage some students from contributing and participating. I bring up this last challenge just because we have all seen how fragile a student looks when she or he dares to speak up for the first time. I certainly tend to provide extra reinforcement. In using the QFT, I realize the process itself creates the space for the students to emerge on their own, so I try to reduce their need for being validated by me.

TRY IT!

I hope the challenges I've talked about here don't discourage you from trying the QFT. It really becomes second nature pretty quickly, and that goes for the students as well. Now, when I give them an assignment, tell them to go observe something, or take notes, soon I'll hear, "But, can we also ask questions?" That's quite a change. And I see how the practice is helping them in other areas as well: they can start a writing assignment on their own, they're understanding more from readings I give them—especially if we've done the QFT before entering a new area.

I've seen that giving my students a chance to learn how to ask their own questions is giving them a powerful tool for becoming self-directed learners. I strongly encourage you to try it, knowing full well that there can be some challenges. Let me know what happens. I've enjoyed sharing notes on the process. And have fun. I sure do.

CHAPTER 10

Students and Classrooms Transformed

A Community of Self-Directed Learners

"I gained a higher and more extensive knowledge about making inferences and questioning the text and understanding my own perspective."

"You can't learn unless you ask questions. Unless you ask questions, nobody knows what you are thinking or what you want to know."

THE SEVENTEENTH-CENTURY BRITISH STATESMAN, scientist, and philosopher Francis Bacon, who advanced the idea of the scientific method, said: "Who questions much, shall learn much, and retain much." Centuries later, one of the students quoted at the beginning of this chapter made pretty much the same argument: "You can't learn unless you ask questions." Students report and teachers see abundant evidence of deeper learning when the QFT is used in the classroom. But it's also a phenomenon we all can recognize in ourselves without any experience in the QFT. If we have asked a question about a subject or concern, we are much better attuned to the information coming back to us. We are, therefore, more likely to retain it. Information that is simply delivered to us when we haven't asked for it can fly right by, and we don't give it a moment's thought.

When students return to look at an original Question Focus thirty minutes, three days, or three weeks after they first encountered it, they are coming back to a familiar place, something they have seen before. But they see it now in an entirely different light. In his series of poems "Four Quartets," T.S. Eliot captured this kind of transformation with these lines:

We shall not cease from exploration
And the end of all our exploring
Will be to arrive where we started
And know the place for the first time.

The students have gone exploring and traveled along their own line of inquiry, followed the lead of their questions, and worked on those questions. They have returned to exactly where they "started" and now "know the place" in a way they never could have imagined when they began.

CHANGES IN STUDENTS

The changes resulting from using the QFT are noticeable. Students name three categories of changes in themselves:

- They have gained a better understanding of content and greater learning.
- They have gained confidence, become self-starters, are more engaged, and take ownership of their own learning.
- They have developed lifelong thinking skills to use in their education and beyond.

Better Understanding of Content and Greater Learning

Students frequently report that going through the questioning process "helped me think a lot" and that as a result, "I understand now more than I did before." The questions, seen at first as a detour from getting information (either delivered to them by teacher or acquired through their own research), wind up offering a shortcut to new understanding. A high school math teacher told us that when students go from producing their own questions all the way to prioritizing them, "they retain information better because they own it. And every teacher wants to help students retain information, because when [the students] remember their questions and then get the information, it's like they recognize it as what *they* wanted to know. They say: 'Oh yeah, yeah, that's what I was looking for.'"

Ling-Se Peet's summer school students who were at risk of being held back were asked what they thought about learning to ask their own questions (see figure 10.1 for a breakdown of responses). A quarter of them reported that the question formulation process was valuable because "it's important to know" how to ask your own questions. Nearly double that number, 48 percent, reported that going through the whole process specifically helped them learn more from the reading assignments and better understand the lesson. They also wrote that it helps because:

- "You can understand and get everything out of the information you just learned."
- "It helps you understand the material."
- "It helps you understand what you are reading or talking about."
- "The more you ask questions the more thoughts come to your head and it helps expand your learning."
- "When I ask questions, it helps me by knowing at what I am studying through my own perspective. It allows me to question myself as well as the subject."

FIGURE 10.1

Ninth-grade summer school classroom end-of-program assessment: Students name the *primary* outcome of learning to ask their own questions

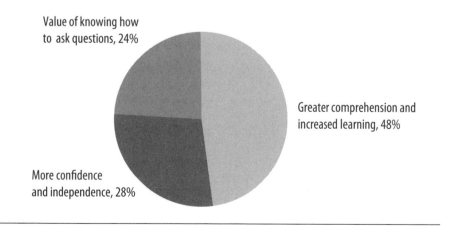

Then one student, showing how the questioning process becomes a direct aid in traditional learning activities, commented: "Because when you ask questions and if you get answers [it] will help you memorize what you asked and the answer."

Laurie Gaughran, in her history class at Humanities Prep, aims to give her students the skills to think for themselves. She uses the QFT regularly to help these youth—many of whom have struggled in other schools—read challenging texts, engage with big ideas, and prepare and write essays. When asked what value they found in the QFT, 70 percent of her students talked about how it helped improve their thinking, learning and understanding of the topic (see figure 10.2). One of her students wrote that he had "learned that asking questions helps us receive a deeper understanding of a topic. We're not just randomly talking about a topic, we are answering questions that we can answer for each other. It helps us go in depth about a topic."

More Engaged Students Who Take Ownership of Their Learning

One teacher reports that students loved doing what they described as "question-storming" and now want to do it at the start of every new unit. In Ariela Rothstein's

FIGURE 10.2

Urban high school history class: Students name the *primary* value of the question formulation technique

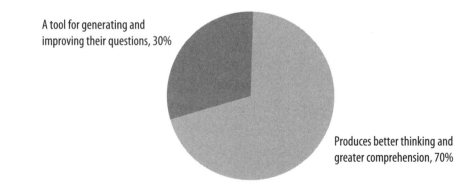

A tool for generating and improving their questions, 30%

Produces better thinking and greater comprehension, 70%

government class at East Brooklyn Community High School, the students—who struggled in early attempts to ask their own questions—began to use their new skill as a way to approach any assignment. Instructed to take notes on what they observed in a Norman Rockwell painting representing "freedom of speech," several of the students lobbied, just a few minutes into the assignment, for expanding the instructions: "Can we ask questions about what we're seeing?"

Students express again and again that questions are now the vehicle for driving their own learning, "because when you ask your own questions you're basically challenging yourself." Another student put out this maxim for learning: "In order to learn beyond your knowledge, ask questions to further the mind." Another student, agreed, talking about how asking questions will help her "expand my ideas" and how, in the future, she will be able to "make my own questions and teach myself what I need to know."

The ability to ask questions is a muscle that, once developed, gets used—and by being used, gets stronger. It is similar to Oliver Wendell Holmes' observation that: "A mind once stretched by a new idea never regains its original dimension." The stretching of the new muscle builds confidence as students, especially struggling ones, take advantage of the space created by the rules for producing questions to initiate new lines of thinking. Charlese Harris, at Boston Day and Evening Academy, observed: "Students who think they are not smart ask the better questions, once they see their questions are not being judged or criticized." This was confirmed by her colleague Sara Fass, who reported: "It's amazing to see how the kids who think they're smart struggle to come up with questions and the ones who don't see themselves as smart came up with some amazing questions."

The more all students practice, the more they feel, as one student proudly reported to Ling-Se Peet at the end of the summer school program: "I'm getting good at this question thing." The smile on his face when he realized that and said it was contagious. Other students add to the evidence of the changes they note in themselves:

- "I was fast and asked good questions."
- "I can phrase and write questions differently."
- "My ability to ask questions is very different from before I never asked questions."

And, of course, as the student in Peet's summer school class put it, knowing how to ask questions makes her "feel smart."

Lifelong Thinking Skills to Use in the Classroom and Beyond

The students at J. L. Stanford Middle School in Palo Alto were quick to point out the value of learning how to ask questions (see figure 10.3). Many of them also volunteered that they saw value not only for immediate work but for future projects and assignments as well. One student said that having a process for asking her own questions "is a great way to form project ideas. I ended up asking questions that I never would have thought of before." One of her classmates echoed her discovery, saying that she "could use that process again when brainstorming for almost any project. It would work best when coming up with how to turn a big topic into a smaller, more specific one." One student thought about her English class and said: "I could use that process on my own while writing. Although it would be different, I could ask myself questions about my plot and characters and decide on a story."

Many students quickly see the ramifications of knowing how to ask their own questions in their lives beyond school. High school students in Boston commented frequently about using their new skills "to talk to adults" and to "help me get a job."

FIGURE 10.3

Suburban middle school: Students name the *primary* value of the Question Formulation Technique

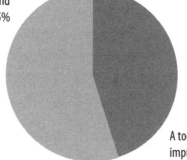

Produces better thinking and greater comprehension, 55%

A tool for generating and improving their questions, 45%

The knowledge of how to re-create a learning process stimulated many students to imagine ways they could use the skill. One sixth-grader wrote: "I will use this in my future years of being Darwin Jr. because I will probably have to come up with some famous theories."

CHANGES IN CLASSROOMS

The students notice the changes in themselves when they use the Question Formulation Technique. They may not realize that the teachers and their schools are also noticing significant differences in their academic and social behavior. There are three general categories of the changes that can be seen in classroom effectiveness. The QFT:

- Increases participation in group and peer learning processes
- Improves classroom management
- Enhances classroom practices to address inequities in education

Improved Participation in Group and Peer Learning Processes

The QFT gives students a very structured, yet open process for allowing them to learn from each other. It's a balancing act, but the process allows for a period in which only the generation of questions is allowed, and another portion where students can discuss the relative values of different questions as they try to prioritize them. Students take notice of the group process, with some students reporting that they like "working in groups" and that "we had a really good discussion." One student reported that hearing other questions "made me think a lot," adding: "I liked the process because I could see a lot of ideas. I could also see other peoples' ideas instead of just my ideas. My group got a great topic which led to us getting a lot of information."

One student picked up on one aspect of the process in particular: the use of the Rules for Producing Questions to create a more open, tolerant process. He noted, "I liked how any ideas could be put down. This way, there is no conflict about whether or not it is a 'bad idea.' Also it makes it so that the group doesn't pass up something that would be great with a little tweaking."

The process lends itself to students helping each other climb a pretty steep learning curve relatively quickly. One teacher saw these comments as part of a larger phenomenon: "I was struck by how learning to formulate questions in a group setting can build teamwork, listening, and communication skills too."

Better Classroom Management

The QFT was not designed with this in mind, but teachers have observed that it can work well to help a class learn to regulate itself. Teachers often note that the nuanced back-and-forth between structure and open space, between clear teacher directions and room for a strong student voice, leads to more energized and self-disciplined classrooms.

The Rules for Producing Questions help a lot, especially because their introduction at the beginning of the process is preceded by a student discussion of why it might be difficult to keep to the rules. That discussion can intrigue students because they have a chance to name problems that might come up, recognize them when they do surface, and then refer back to the rules to keep themselves from discussing, judging, or making statements. The rules go from serving as a teacher-enforced discipline to a student-owned process for regulating their own behavior. The system doesn't always work perfectly, but it creates a climate of high expectations and greater student ownership—those two magical pieces of a successful classroom.

The QFT also makes clear that there will be specific outcomes (a list of questions, changed questions, prioritized questions) and the students will be held accountable by a public presentation of their questions to other groups in the classroom. When a time limit is added to these specific outcomes, the students know what they need to deliver, when they will deliver, and to whom. The QFT thus turns the responsibility for outcomes over to a group of students. Of course, some students resist it. They are accustomed to traditional question-and-response methods between teachers and students that reinforce a message many students have internalized—that their only job is to respond when they are called upon. At all other times, they either feel license to, or take liberties to disengage from the learning process or pester other students. The structure of the QFT, the reporting to their peers, and the teacher reminders to complete the assigned task give them far less license to do so. As we have seen all over the country, the process takes over and some of the most recalcitrant students are pulled in and become active contributors.

An Effective Strategy for Engaging and Working with At-Risk Students

The QFT offers an unusual combination of features that works for all students on all levels. It is a rare example of an approach that can push successful students to think more deeply and can also be used to engage and stimulate new thinking among struggling students. The technique provides:

- A clear, disciplined structure
- Open space for different student learning and talking styles
- Respect for student ideas and ability to work together
- High expectations that students can think at very high levels

The ninth-graders in Ling-Se Peet's summer school class, at risk of being held back a year, struggled at first with the process. Some students had trouble staying in their seats, or even in their groups, preferring to wander over to another group, not necessarily to check on their questions, but to get the attention of one of that group's members. Some students didn't get what they were supposed to do—the process had never been asked of them before—and tried to disengage.

By the second time they went through the QFT process, the change in their behavior and practice was striking. They recognized the practice, seemed to enjoy the opportunity to think together, and only occasionally got distracted by random exchanges about their preferences for Usher over Eminem or 50 Cent. They got by with a little help from their friends, and from the teacher—and wound up staying on task. By the end of the five-week summer school program, 87 percent of the students named the ability to ask questions as the most important and useful thing they learned during their summer remedial class: of these, 50 percent specifically named the Question Formulation Technique, while another 37 percent described learning in general to "ask questions" as the most important thing. Only three of the twenty-four students in the class (13 percent) did not mention either asking questions or the QFT (see figure 10.4).

Ariela Rothstein's class at East Brooklyn Community High School (EBCHS) includes many students who have transferred from other schools where they struggled or have aged out of school. She deliberately builds the QFT into the middle of a two-week teaching unit. When students were preparing for a moot court exercise, she designed the QFocus described in chapter 2: "Miranda rights always protects the rights of the accused."

FIGURE 10.4

Ninth-grade summer school classroom end-of-program assessment: Students reflect on the *most important lesson* **they learned by participating in the five-week summer school program**

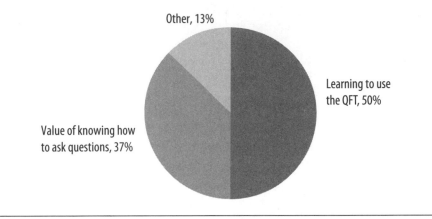

Other, 13%

Learning to use the QFT, 50%

Value of knowing how to ask questions, 37%

Her students were energized by the questions they developed, which touched on themes of justice, equity, personal and public responsibility, public institutions, and, of course, the rights of all people. Rothstein's use of the QFT is seen by some colleagues as a "classroom management" tool, since students are more engaged when using it than they are in other teaching and learning exercises. Rothstein sees its potential as a tool for helping students discover just how capable they are of thinking for themselves; a message not many have heard in their schooling. As a result of her work, EBCHS has set "Questioning Historical Content" as a specific outcome that can be measured in her courses. This is official recognition of the value of student questions and allows them to be recognized for their ability to ask them.

At the Boston Day and Evening Academy, a school similar in purpose to EBCHS, Yana Minchenko and Rachel Jean-Marie found that they could design a curriculum in their humanities class that managed to do two things at once that were very important for their particular student population:

- The simple QFocus, "The choices we make," was directly related to a short story the students were reading that was very relevant to the students' own struggles, which could affect their choices about staying in school.

- The student-generated questions could drive the writing process as the students learned how to write short responses and essays.

Teachers working in environments where students struggle and are at risk of dropping out or failing (and thus getting on a path toward dropping out) can use the QFT to give the students the abilities and skills to become agents able to think and act more effectively on their own behalf. It can be a major contribution to directly addressing the challenges in schools serving these at-risk students.

When Ling-Se Peet reflected on what she had learned by using the QFT with her summer school class, she thought about how the process had managed to engage and stimulate African American and Latino male students in ways that nothing else had ever quite done. The process worked for the young women in the class as well, offering them opportunities to take on a range of leadership roles in the small groups, but, she was particularly struck by how the young men seemed to thrive when given responsibility for their own learning and a clear process to use to do it. The changes began with "increased confidence in their ability to use the QFT, a deeper understanding of what closed- and open-ended questions are, and a greater willingness to ask questions during class (even when we weren't doing the QFT)."

One of Peet's students displayed all of these kinds of changes. During the first week of summer school, she would almost never raise her hand to participate, but by the end of summer school she was the leader in her QFT group, clarifying what an open-ended and closed-ended question was for her classmates who weren't sure and volunteering to read her questions aloud. This is the same student who had come to "feel smart" by learning to ask her own questions.

Another student, who had generally just quietly disengaged before, "used to act out and misbehave during the first week of summer school." As he began to take charge of his own learning in the QFT, he changed. "By the last week he was focused, attentive, and raising his hand to ask questions, even when we weren't doing the QFT."

The examples of these two young students made Peet "think about the powerful implications that the QFT has for bridging the achievement gap for minority male students." She believes that "they showed these improvements because they felt empowered by the QFT." At the Boston Day and Evening Academy, math teacher Charlese Harris had found a creative way to use the QFT—presenting "The

Quadratic Formula" as the QFocus—and was struck by the questions her class generated and the degree to which these students were readier to learn after going through the process. "In a math class," she said, "students are expecting to be told what to do, and not expecting to think for themselves." In previous work at the Algebra Project, Harris hoped to help students find their way to successful educational outcomes.[1] She has seen, however "that many of the students of color in my community display a passive resistance to school and to learning. I understand where they are coming from, but in the end, it doesn't help them. The QFT offers a way for them to own the learning process themselves. It could be revolutionary."

Sharif Muhammad has taught at BDEA for seven years, helping students do independent "capstone" projects related to career exploration. He encourages students to generate questions and has seen just how difficult it can be for them. When he began to use the QFT, he was struck by "how they went farther and deeper and did it more quickly than ever before." One student, Pedro, looked at psychology as a career option and generated a full eighteen questions, beginning with "Is it a safe job?" and concluding with "Is it a good paying job?" He also chose these priority questions from the ones he generated in between (the seventh, eleventh, and seventeenth):

- What are the requirements and challenges in becoming a psychologist?
- What part of the brain controls people's actions and emotions?
- How would people feel to have a Hispanic male as a psychologist?

At the end of the process, Muhammad asked Pedro to reflect on why learning to ask his own questions is important for learning. Pedro responded: "It is important for learning because you can narrow down all the questions that you have and get the most information out of them."

He went on to talk about how he enjoyed narrowing down the questions and that in the future, he would "start any assignment by writing down questions." Pedro understood that the first step would be to engage in this divergent thinking before moving to convergent thinking—narrowing down the questions. And he was fully ready to do metacognitive thinking—analyzing what he had learned, how he had learned it, and what he could do with what he learned. He articulates very succinctly what the cognitive psychologist Ann Brown emphasized: if students are unaware of why and how they can use the skill they are learning, it is not likely they will transfer their newly acquired skills to a different task.[2]

Pedro's comments capture the appeal of the question formulation process for so many students: it helps them take concrete steps to break down big, overwhelming topics and come up with a plan of action. They show themselves and their teachers that they can do this on their own and then, they own it.

It is worth dwelling for a moment on this accomplishment. The students see themselves in this way and their teachers perceive the transformation as well. This is the direct outcome of using the QFT: students as skilled thinkers and self-directed, motivated, and independent learners.

Questions and Education, Questions and Democracy

*"When you ask questions, you just learn more.
It makes me feel smart."*

*"Now, I know I need to ask questions.
And now I can do it. I never asked questions before."*

W E WANT ALL STUDENTS TO BECOME ACTIVE AND SUCCESSFUL LEARNERS even though we know there is no silver bullet that will produce that outcome. There is no magic wand that will, with one flick of the wrist, remove all the challenges—inside and outside the classroom—that impede student learning.

The absence of a miracle cure leads to endless discussions of how to solve the problems in our schools and frequent debates about the importance of management structures, decision-making authority, teacher preparation, teacher assessments, student achievement, testing practices, and test scores. In the midst of these often-contentious exchanges, we should not lose sight of the fact that no matter where we stand on the ideological spectrum, we all want to see this outcome: students who learn more, take ownership of their learning, and demonstrate that they know more than they did before entering our classrooms.

This book provides evidence of how schools, teachers, and students can move toward that outcome. The lessons gleaned from the students and teachers who appeared in previous chapters allow us to conclude with these three points:

- We can take action today to improve education in every classroom in every school by teaching all students how to ask their own questions.
- Teachers who teach their students how to ask their own questions will feel greater satisfaction and see better results.
- We will create a more well-informed citizenry and a stronger, more vibrant democratic society by teaching all students to ask their own questions.

In the absence of one simple, perfect solution, and given the complexity and seeming intractability of the many problems facing our schools, we should at least seriously consider an Occam's razor solution—a modest, simple approach that goes a long way to producing the optimal results we want. The Question Formulation Technique is a tool that equalizes opportunity for all students while also challenging each individual student to do more than he or she may have thought possible. Its value has been demonstrated for students with parents who help them with their homework every night as well as for students with parents who cannot read the instructions that come with the homework. It works for students who arrive at school having already eaten a full breakfast and it works for students who come to school for their one guaranteed meal a day.

IMPROVING EDUCATION THROUGH DISCOVERY, ENGAGEMENT, AND ACHIEVEMENT

Perhaps the Question Formulation Technique sounds too good to be true, as if it belongs in a late-night infomercial. But it *is* as good as advertised. The first round of evidence for its value comes from the students and teachers you met in these chapters. One middle school student in Palo Alto shared a precious moment of discovery sparked by using the Question Formulation Technique: "Just when you think you already know the question you want to focus on for a project, and you want to get right to it, you spend just a little more time asking questions and all of a sudden you realize: 'Oh, wow, here's this other question that is so much better and that's really what you need to think about.'" A high school student in Boston felt more engaged than ever in her studies, saying, "When you ask the question, you feel like it's your job to get the answer, and you want to figure it out." And, a ninth-grade summer school student realized he now actually understands more than he did before because "when you ask questions, you just learn more about what you're doing in class."

All students in all schools deserve the opportunity to feel what these three students articulated: a profound sense of *discovery, engagement,* and *achievement.* We want more students to experience the burst of energy that comes from asking questions that lead to making new connections, feel a greater sense of urgency to seek answers to questions on their own, and reap the satisfaction of actually understanding more deeply the subject matter as a result of the questions they asked.

If we want students to learn how to ask their own questions, starting today, we need more teachers like the ones in this book who will make that happen. It is far more likely that more teachers will begin to do that if we do something that is not usually done for teachers: make it easier, not harder, for them to teach.

STUDENT QUESTIONS AND BETTER TEACHING

Teachers who have taught their students how to ask their own questions report that they have become better at their craft. Beatriz McConnie-Zapater, Boston Day and Evening Academy's head of school, has seen teachers in her school "sharpen their focus on what is essential to teach" and become "more deliberate in teaching habits of mind" while using the QFT's rigorous scaffolded process. Her teachers recognize a clear before-and-after effect of students "asking more questions" or "going further and deeper with their questions" or being "more active and taking more ownership" than they had ever done before. As one teacher said: "Using the QFT makes me a better teacher as the students learn that it is their job, not mine, to do the heavy lifting of real thinking."

Her observations are confirmed by many other teachers who use the QFT in their classrooms. They see students who can make more sense of what they are studying, retain more information, throw out irrelevant data, uncover new meanings, and discover overlooked connections. They understand more as a result, and carry out better projects, execute more complete experiments, write better essays, and generate solutions to complex math problems. These are profoundly important and exciting educational outcomes.

Learning to ask questions will also help students meet the standards set for them. Standards, as Mike Rose has written, can be seen as legitimate and reasonable expectations for students.[1] The standards we set, he cautions us, should keep in mind the dynamic that John Dewey observed between subject or discipline on one hand and the development of the mind of the student on the other.[2] Standards do not have to equate to rote regurgitation of information. Indeed, there are many ways to set standards that represent clear and high expectations for students. The ability to ask questions has helped the students in this book meet higher expectations.

Deborah Meier has argued that "the art of good teaching begins when we can answer the questions our students are really trying to ask us, *if only they knew how to do so.*"[3] (emphasis added) Good teaching as Meier describes it would, we believe, be enhanced by the QFT, which demonstrates that students can indeed learn how to ask their own questions. If good teaching requires, as Meier implies, divining and extracting the unformed question from students' minds, better teaching would insure that students will not depend on the teacher to articulate their questions for them. They can do it themselves.

If students are to do it themselves, if they are to learn how to ask questions, the teaching of the skill should be made an explicit goal in all classrooms. The cognitive psychologist Robert Sternberg, who has done pioneering work on how to broaden and enrich assessment of student achievement, has recently made precisely that point in an analysis of the problematic measures used in college admissions. He believes that schools do indeed need to teach students how to ask questions because "if we always give students the questions, and demand only the answers, we teach them to answer prefabricated questions rather than to ask questions worth asking."[4]

The need is clear and the goal is noble, but moving to a model of teaching students to ask their own questions will require a small but significant shift in practice. When first making this just one change, both teacher and student experience a striking reversal of roles. It is a change so simple and yet so profound that it quickly pushed Ling-Se Peet to think in new ways about "what student-centered learning really looks like." Seeing her students actively engaged in producing and then using their questions offered a glimpse of just how much learning can take place when students take on the responsibility of driving their own learning.

Students who acquire that new sense of responsibility for their own learning are starting down a path that can lead them to another arena where they could also act on a sense of responsibility as a citizen in a democracy.

STUDENTS LEARNING TO ASK QUESTIONS CAN MAKE DEMOCRACY WORK BETTER

The philosophical terrain connecting education to democracy has been well traveled for more than a century, and the need for an informed citizenry was recognized early in American history. Philosophy and aspirations aside, how can we improve the daily practice of education for democracy?

It is no simple matter. Democracy is, after all, a risky, complicated enterprise. In ancient Greece, the elders of Athens thought democratic rights should be limited to relatively few men among the total population. When we consider just one aspect of democracy—voting—we see how much effort goes into restricting rather than expanding the franchise. When our country was founded, only male property holders were given the right to vote. Women had to wait a full century and a half or so before being able to cast a ballot. Entire state administrations mobilized to prevent African American citizens from voting up until the second half of the twentieth century.

More voices and more participation can indeed complicate matters. Winston Churchill once described democracy as the worst form of government except for all others that have been tried. Why, then, would we want to invite more people to start exercising the very democratic practice of asking questions? Because we don't want the alternatives referred to by Churchill. A monarchy or a dictatorship can rule and survive for too many decades by making it difficult for anyone to ask questions and think independently. What is good for a dictatorship should be considered bad for a democracy.

Even in our democratic society, we have not done a particularly good job of investing in developing our citizens' ability to think independently and ask their own questions. We need to make a stronger, more deliberate effort to build the capacity of all our citizens to think for themselves, weigh evidence, discern between fact and myth, discuss, debate, analyze, and prioritize. In twenty years of work with The Right Question Institute in a wide range of communities, we have seen how much can be accomplished when people who never before participated in decisions affecting them on any level begin to ask their own questions and acquire democratic habits of mind.

We have occasionally heard from highly educated people that there really is no need to make that investment, to actually teach people how to ask their own questions. They respond to hearing about the work of the Right Question Institute with either a shrug: "Surely all people know how to do that," or skepticism: "It really isn't that important to spend time deliberately teaching people how to ask their own questions." Their indifferent responses represent an assumption or bias that is mirrored as well in much of the debate about how to improve education for all students; the idea of teaching students to ask their own questions does not show up as even the tiniest blip on the radar screen of education reform.

The ability to ask questions may be taken for granted by highly educated people, just as asking questions as a democratic habit of mind may be taken for granted by people who have lived their entire lives in societies where they have the freedom to ask questions. But, the profound significance of being able to ask questions is not missed by people who have suffered from the absence of democracy. For example, Abraham Joshua Heschel, a rabbi and scholar who was a refugee from Nazi Germany, asserted at a White House Conference on Children and Youth in 1960 that in a democratic society we should be assessing our students less on their ability to answer our questions and more on their ability to ask their own questions.[5] The educator Paolo Freire was actually thrown in jail by a dictatorship in his native Brazil for challenging its authority and then spent much of his life after that challenging societies around the world to embrace questions and questioning as a fundamental democratic action.

The need to deliberately teach democratic skills can surprise recent visitors to this country. One group of leaders of non-governmental organizations in the newly democratic countries of the former Soviet Bloc came to the United States more than a decade ago and were surprised to discover that there was even a need for an organization like The Right Question Institute. They asked in amazement: "Don't citizens know they have the right to ask questions and participate in decisions?"

Many students do indeed learn in the course of studying American history and government that they have the *right* to ask questions. But that is not enough. We should also deliberately develop their *ability* to ask questions. If we use the QFT methodology, they will also begin to develop a range of democratic habits that prepare them to do something we see done far too rarely by their elders: work together.

Beatriz McConnie-Zapater has noted these additional positive results when students work on their questions in small groups. "You can have a meeting of the minds, and you can also argue, discuss, debate, and contribute new thinking about an idea. This is, after all, a prerequisite to constructing a more just and democratic society." The open but rigorous structure of the QFT allows students to constantly practice and hone democratic habits. The students listen to each other's questions, learn from each other, discuss and debate, consider different kinds of information required, and determine the sequence in which they need that information. And, they have to work together to find a way, be it by voting or through consensus, to select their priority questions.

Each time they use the Question Formulation Technique, students put their intellects through a serious workout and at the same time, often unbeknownst to them, they are engaged as well in a vigorous democratic process and action on a micro level. "When you ask questions," as a student in Ms. Peet's class observed when thinking about governmental actions, "it helps you think not just about what is done, but also about what should or could be done by all of us."

The more often students use the Question Formulation Technique, the more practiced they become in the ways of democratic deliberation. In your classroom, you can, at a time of your choosing, make this visible to them so that they become just as aware of the democratic implications of their intellectual labors as they do of its academic purpose.

A CALL TO ACTION

We must make an investment in cultivating democratic habits of mind if we want citizens to be able to participate in democracy. Democracy, Amy Gutmann—political philosopher and now president of the University of Pennsylvania—has argued, "depends on democratic education for its full moral strength."[6] We all need our students to grow more comfortable with democratic habits of mind and action. They live in a society in which barely 60 percent of the total eligible population actually votes—nearly four out of every ten citizens do not participate even at the high tide of voting in hotly contested presidential elections. We should not be surprised. Too often, ordinary citizens as well as students are expected to come over to some other place to participate in democracy. We are missing opportunity after opportunity for people to begin to act democratically where they are, in their daily experiences.

We developed the new concept of *microdemocracy* to draw attention to the importance of individual citizens learning to participate in decisions that affect them, beginning on the level closest to them.[7]

Teachers, because of their direct access to students, can become real democracy builders—not in a clichéd sort of way, but rather by teaching students to ask their own questions, an essential democratic as well foundational thinking skill. You and your students will see the benefits immediately in the classroom, and they will reap the benefits for the long haul. And so will we all benefit as they become more active and informed citizens and join efforts in this country and beyond to build and maintain the democratic structure that affords all citizens the right to ask questions.

We invite you to join the community of teachers you met in this book to produce the next round of evidence of how we can enhance learning, improve teaching, and strengthen democracy when all students have the opportunity to learn to ask their own questions.

Notes

Introduction

1. All student names used in this book are pseudonyms. Actual names are used for all adults and for grade and school information.
2. For more information on the origins of the Question Formulation Technique see: http://www.rightquestion.org/about/history.
3. A Socratic seminar is a method in which guiding questions are presented to students to help promote dialogue and discussion.
4. For more information on the work of The Right Question Institute, see www.rightquestion.org.
5. Margarita Alegría, PhD., et al., "Evaluation of a Patient Activation and Empowerment Intervention in Mental Health Care," *Medical Care* 46, no. 3 (2008): 247–256; Darwin Deen, Wei-Hsin Lu, Dan Rothstein, Luz Santana, and Marthe R. Gold, "Asking Questions: The Effect of a Brief Intervention in Community Health Centers on Patient Activation," *Patient Education and Counseling* August 25, 2010 (online publication ahead of print; http://www.pec-journal.com/article/S0738-3991(10)00427-1/abstract).
6. These comments, shared by teachers Susan Bupp and Shirley Jackson, can be heard on the video "Why Didn't I Learn This in High School?" at http://www.rightquestion.org/resources/videos).
7. Kathryn Parker Boudett, Elizabeth A. City, and Richard J. Murnane, eds., *Data Wise: A Step-by-Step Guide to Using Assessment Results to Improve Teaching and Learning.* (Cambridge, MA: Harvard Education Press, 2005).
8. Richard J. Murnane and Frank Levy, *Teaching the New Basic Skills: Principles for Educating Children in a Changing Economy* (New York: Basic Books, 1996).

Chapter 1

1. *A note on sequence:* The Right Question Institute and the Question Formulation Technique (QFT) emerged from years of direct work in low-income communities around the country. The QFT is a teaching and learning methodology that developed organically and only later did we find its value "named" in more academic terms. The QFT did not emerge from a research project that was turned into a curriculum. Once the methodology was fully developed, we learned that there is an extensive literature in cognitive science, psychology, and educational and pedagogical theory that articulates the kinds of thinking abilities that people acquire by using the QFT.

The research on how people learn to think for themselves would be helpful to anyone interested in a more in-depth exploration of the ideas presented here. We suggest as a starting place a report produced by the National Research Council: John D. Bransford, Ann L. Brown, and Rodney R. Cocking, eds., *How People Learn: Brain, Mind, Experience and School* (Washington, DC: National Academies Press, 2000).

For good sources of both theory and practical information on developing cognitive skills, see Robert J. Sternberg and Louise Spear-Swerling, *Teaching for Thinking* (Washington, DC: American Psychological Association, 1996), and the work of Ann Palincsar. For an extensive analysis of various approaches for teaching thinking and cognitive skills, see: Raymond S. Nickerson David N. Perkins, and Edward E. Smith, *The Teaching of Thinking* (Hillsdale, NJ: Lawrence Erlbaum, 1985). For sources on the importance of children being engaged in their own exploration and question-asking, see Eleanor Duckworth's *The Having of Wonderful Ideas and Other Essays on Teaching and Learning*, 3rd ed. (New York: Teachers College Press, 2006); For a valuable source on teaching adults with limited education to think for themselves, see Jane Vella, *Learning to Listen, Learning to Teach: The Power of Dialogue in Educating Adults* (San Francisco: Jossey-Bass, 1994).

2. For more detailed descriptions on the definitions of divergent thinking, see, for example, Oh Nam Kwon, Jung Sook Park, and Jee Hyun Park, "Cultivating Divergent Thinking in Mathematics Through an Open-Ended Approach." *Asia Pacific Education Review* 7, no.1 (2006): 51–61.

3. For research regarding divergent thinking in various age groups and settings, see Mary Jo Puckett Cliatt, Jean M. Shaw, and Jeanne M. Sherwood, "Effects of Training on the Divergent-Thinking Abilities of Kindergarten Children," *Child Development* 51, no. 4 (1980): 1061–1064. Also see D. Souza Fleith, J. S. Renzulli, and K. L. Westberg, "Effects of a Creativity Training Program on Divergent Thinking Abilities and Self-Concept in Monolingual and Bilingual Classrooms," *Creativity Research Journal* 14, nos. 3–4 (2002): 373–386.

4. Christophe Mouchiroud and Todd Lubart, "Children's Original Thinking: an Empirical Examination of Alternative Measures Derived from Divergent Thinking Tasks," *Journal of Genetic Psychology* 162, no. 4 (2001): 382–401; Mark A. Runco, "Flexibility and Originality in Children's Divergent Thinking," *Journal of Psychology* 120, no. 4 (1986): 345–352.

5. Runco, "Flexibility and Originality in Children's Divergent Thinking."

6. Po Bronson and Ashley Merryman, "The Creativity Crisis," *Newsweek*, July 10, 2010.

7. A.Vincent Ciardiello, "Did You Ask a Good Question Today? Alternative Cognitive and Metacognitive Strategies," *Journal of Adolescent & Adult Literacy* 42, no. 3 (1998): 210–219.

8. Bronson and Merryman, "The Creativity Crisis."

9. Ann L.Brown and Joseph C. Campione, "Guided Discovery in a Community of Learners," in *Classroom Lessons: Integrating Cognitive Theory and Classroom Practice*, ed. Kate McGilly (Cambridge, MA: MIT Press, 1994), 229–272.

10. Ann L. Brown, "Knowing When, Where, and How to Remember: A Problem of Metacognition," in *Advances In Instructional Psychology*, vol. 1, ed. R. Glaser (Hillsdale, NJ: Erlbaum, 1978): 77–165.

11. Bransford, Brown, and Cocking, *How People Learn.*

12. Linda Baker, "Metacognition," Gale Group, 2003, http://www.education.com/reference/article/metacognition/.

13. Milton Schwebel, Charles A. Maher, and Nancy S. Fagley, eds., *Promoting Cognitive Growth Over the Life Span* (Hillsdale, NJ: L. Erlbaum Associates, 1990); Margaret Matlin, *Cognition*, 6th ed. (New York: J. Wiley & Sons, 2005).

14. Matlin, *Cognition*; James L. McClelland and Robert S. Siegler, eds., *Mechanisms of Cognitive Development: Behavioral and Neural Perspectives* (Mahwah, NJ: Lawrence Erlbaum, 2000).

15. Bransford, Brown, and Cocking, *How People Learn.*

Chapter 2

1. The Religious Dimensions of the Torture Debate," Pew poll, April 2009.

2. This speech was given on January 15, 2004, at the Beacon Theater in New York.

Chapter 3

1. Dongbin Lü, *The Secret of the Golden Flower: A Chinese Book of Life*, trans. Richard Wilhelm (London: Routlage, 1999). Jung's comment about just how difficult it is to produce something simple also is relevant to how the Rules for Producing Questions differ from a traditional brainstorming process for generating a lot of ideas while withholding judgment. There is something very different about the seemingly simple act of asking questions that requires a specific set of rules to overcome the obstacles to producing questions.

2. Elliot Forbes, Lewis Lockwood, Donald Martino, and Bernard Rands, "Faculty of Arts and Sciences Memorial Minute: Earl Kim," *Harvard University Gazette*, May 25, 2000.

3. Statement made by Rebecca Steinitz; at Right Question professional development workshop, Boston Day and Evening Academy, May 5, 2010.

Chapter 6

1. Sarah Spinks, "Teenage Brains Are a Work in Progress," http://www.pbs.org/wgbh/pages/frontline/shows/teenbrain/work/adolescent.html#ixzz1KCIHzta4.

2. Original thinking and new discoveries are often preceded by going down the wrong path. The physicist Edward Witten considered to be Einstein's successor at the Institute for Advanced Studies, said, "If you are a researcher you are trying to figure out what the question is as well as what the answer is. You want to find the question that is sufficiently easy that you might be able to answer it, and sufficiently hard that the answer is interesting. You spend a lot of time thinking and you spend a lot of time floundering around," http://edition.cnn.com/2005/TECH/science/06/27/witten.physics/index.html

Chapter 7

1. The moot court is a method of teaching in which students argue a hypothetical issue in order to practice legal skills such as analysis of argument from both sides.

2. Clay Shirky, *Cognitive Surplus: Creativity and Generosity in a Connected Age* (New York: Penguin Press, 2010).

3. David Johnston and John M. Broder, "F.B.I. Says Guards Killed 14 Iraqis Without Cause," *New York Times*, November 14, 2007.

Chapter 9

1. The term *zone of proximity* is attributed to developmental psychologist Lev Vygotsky, who defines it as "the distance between the actual development level as determined by independent problem solving and the level of potential under adult guidance or in collaboration with more capable peers"; see "Interaction Between Learning and Development" in *Mind and Society*, eds. Lev Semenovich and Michael Cole (Cambridge, MA: Harvard University Press, 1978), 79–91.
2. KWL is a technique designed to activate a student's prior knowledge. It stands for "what do you *K*now?", "what do you *W*ant to know?", and "what have you *L*earned?"

Chapter 10

1. The Algebra Project was started by the civil rights activist Bob Moses, who argued that the study of algebra by minority students was an extension of the civil rights movement and was essential to their long term success in school.
2. Ann L. Brown, *Knowing When, Where, and How to Remember: A Problem of Metacognition*, Report No. 47, National Institute of Education Center for the Study of Reading (Champaign, IL: National Institute of Education, 1977), 69.

Conclusion

1. Mike Rose. *Why School? Reclaiming Education for All of Us* (New York: The New Press, 2009), 114–115.
2. John Dewey. *Democracy and Education: An Introduction to the Philosophy of Education*, quoted in ibid.
3. Deborah Meier, "Standardization Versus Standards" *Phi Delta Kappan* 84, no. 3 (2002): 197.
4. Robert J. Sternberg. *College Admissions for the 21st Century* (Cambridge, MA: Harvard University Press, 2010), 147–148.
5. Abraham Joshua Heschel, "Children and Youth," paper presented at White House Conference on Youth, March 28, 1960 (published in A. J. Heschel, *The Insecurity of Freedom: Essays on Human Existence* [New York: Schocken Books, 1972], 46–47);The Brazilian educator Paolo Freire is best known for his book, *The Pedagogy of the Oppressed* (New York: Herder and Herder, 1972). See a full discussion about the purposes of education in a democratic society in Paolo Freire and Myles Horton, *We Make the Road by Walking: Conversation on Education and Social Change* (Philadelphia: Temple University Press, 1990).
6. Amy Gutmann, *Democratic Education* (Princeton, NJ: Princeton University Press, 1987), 289.
7. http://www.rightquestion.org/Microdemocracy.

Acknowledgments

It is no simple matter to write a book like this while continuing the ongoing work of a small nonprofit organization operating in many fields and communities. We are deeply grateful to the wide range of people who have made this book possible. Each person named below has provided us with invaluable moral support and encouragement that had more of an impact on us than she or he may know and more than it is possible for us to acknowledge in this brief passage. We hope that those named here read these few words as a very personal thank you from us right now, and as a future thank you from the many teachers and students who will do great things with what they learn from this book.

The support came in many ways and happened on many fronts.

We start with the students and teachers who are at the heart of this book. The students from whom we learned offered us insights, observations, reflections, and products that have greatly enriched this book. We thank them for embracing a new way of thinking and learning and proving themselves to be naturals at it. All teachers, day in and day out, take on an enormous responsibility that is not always fully recognized or appreciated. We want to acknowledge their hard work and the many demands placed on them. We have been particularly inspired by the following teachers who responded eagerly to an opportunity to enrich and strengthen their students' learning experiences and have done masterful work: Amy Alvarez, Hayley Dupuy, Sara Fass, Jimmy Frickey, Angela Gannon, Laurie Gaughran, Charlese Harris, Megan Harvell, Rachel Jean-Marie, Paige Knight, Jennifer Mills, Yanina (Yana) Minchenko, Sharif Muhammad, Lisa Onsum, Marcy Ostberg, Ling-Se Peet, Janet Platt, Ariela Rothstein, Katie Schramm, Aaron Stone, and Joanna Taylor, as well as the many teachers who have participated in workshops at the Coalition of Essential Schools' Fall Forum conferences over the past decade. We also appreciate support from the following principals: Nicole Gittens, Patrick McGillicuddy, and Sharon Ofek.

We had a very special opportunity to work in depth with the great teachers at the Boston Day and Evening Academy. It was made possible by their visionary leader, Beatriz McConnie-Zapater, and supported at the school by Director of Curriculum and Instruction Alison Hramiec and Assistant Head of School Emilys Peña, as well as by Rebecca Steinitz from WriteBoston.

We also appreciate the special efforts made by Martin Sleeper and Margot Stern-Strom, who committed precious senior staff time at Facing History and Ourselves to explore how to introduce our work to their wonderful network of teachers. We are grateful to Max Klau of City Year (and the Selah program that connected us), who introduced our work to idealistic staff and corps members, including Bobby Kessling, Paul Riley, and Christopher Steinkamp. We thank Bill Kovach, former director of the Nieman Foundation for Journalism at Harvard University, Martha Minow, Dean of Harvard Law School, and Wendy Puriefoy, president of the Public Education Network, for their invaluable cheerleading as we wrote this book.

Although this book has the name of two coauthors on its cover, an entire village of an organization has its fingerprints and contributions on many of the inside pages. The Right Question Institute's board of directors approved the writing of this book and steadfastly supported the effort. Veteran board members Agnes Bain, Macky Buck, David Guberman, Ron Walker, and Rick Weissbourd have stayed with us for the long haul, and we are very grateful to them for helping us get to this point. Agnes Bain has been a full and invaluable partner for many years in the development of the Right Question Strategy that is presented in this work. New board members Lavada Berger, Diane Englander, Franklin Fisher, Stephen Quatrano, and Mary Wendell joined us at a critical moment, providing great energy and support with Diane, Mary and David contributing many extra hours over the past year in support of our ongoing work while we were writing this book.

We are deeply grateful to extraordinary educators in the field of adult education who have taught us so much about the usefulness of the Question Formulation Technique for their adult learners in GED and ESOL programs. State adult education directors and leaders from Arizona, Indiana, Maine, Missouri, New Hampshire, New Mexico, Pennsylvania, and Vermont (with the support of Jane's Trust, the Rockefeller Brothers Fund, and the Carnegie Corporation) allowed us ample opportunity to work with their teachers and learn from their adult learners. These people played key roles in making all that possible and have worked alongside us at various points on the journey: Art Ellison, Jennifer Ferrigno, Natasha Freidus, Ami Magisos, Alexandra Piñeros-Shields, and Earldine Tolbert. Patricia Nelson has done all that and more as she has worked closely with us and played a key role in preparing the work for classroom practice. We are grateful, as well, to Jane Vella, who has modeled for us a lifetime of designing educational methods that make it possible for all people to learn and grow.

Stephen Quatrano is a colleague, adviser, and friend to whom we are deeply grateful for his steadfast efforts to encourage us to leverage the full potential of our educational strategy. Richard Murnane at the Harvard Graduate School of Education has generously shared his expertise with practitioners doing the hard work on the frontlines of schools around the country, and has repeatedly sought out ways for our ideas and practice to become part of larger efforts to improve schools for all children. We hope this book will make that easier.

We are grateful for the critical assistance we received from Brian Dugdale and Megan Powell as we first got to work on the book and for additional support later in the process from Gill Benedek and Francesca Pfrommer. Peter Bonnano provided timely and valuable research assistance. We also appreciate the hard work of interns who helped along the way: Becky Eidelman, Dan Kim, Qing Li, Robin Moten, Chelsea Pennucci, Usha Rao, and Tonia Smith. Nadia Nibbs made a special contribution with thoughtful classroom observations and excellent documentation that enhanced our learning. In the past few months, Denise Amisial, Christina Kay, and Valerie Stancil came through early and often at key deadline junctures to cross our t's and dot our i's and save our necks and allow us to get this done. We are grateful to Omri Kahn, whose translations of the Question Formulation Technique into Hebrew helped us clarify and name more clearly the term *Question Focus*.

Early in the project, we also benefited immeasurably from the wise advice of Peter Wissoker, who helped us understand the ways of the publishing world. We were very fortunate to have the wonderful pro bono counsel of Geri Haight at Mintz Levin, who knew, when we didn't, just the right questions to ask.

There would not be a book without the financial resources to support its evolution from idea to reality. We have had the chance to work collaboratively with people from charitable foundations, who start from the position of looking at how to support good work in the field, maximize the difference their grant can make, and then work closely with us to figure out how to best help us get the work done. In chronological order, we are deeply grateful to these people who have been partners in both spirit and action: Stephen Heintz, Ben Shute, and Gail Fuller of the Rockefeller Brothers Fund, John Esterle of The Whitman Institute, and Anne Germanacos of the Germanacos Foundation.

We also had the good fortune to work with major donors who have provided critical support. Diane Englander and Mark Underberg, Franklin and Ellen Fisher, the McLeod Blue Skye Charitable Foundation, Inc., and Mary and Ted Wendell were very nimble and very generous in their responses to our request for help when we had a very small window of opportunity to secure the resources to both write this book and continue the work of The Right Question Institute. We are grateful as well for strong moral and financial support that has meant so much to us over the past year from John Y. Campbell and Susanna Peyton, Mark Barenberg, Laura and Richard Chasin, Susan Cohen and Michael Klein, Evan Eisenberg, Emily Ehrenfeld and Gary Valaskovic, Bob Russman Halperin, John Herron and Julia Moore, Nelson Kravetz (of blessed memory) and Milly Guberman Kravetz, Janny and Jonathan Kravetz, Bernie and Lorraine Horn, Doreen Karroll and Stephen Quatrano, the Kaplun Foundation, Bonnie Orlin, Anne Peretz, Bernie and Sue Pucker, Enid Shapiro, Kay and Stanley Schlozman, Deborah Sinay and Charles Kravetz, Dr. Roslyn Weiner, and Mike and Ruth Worthington. David and Jayne Guberman fit into this category as well and deserve one of their own as founding friends who have been with us from the outset.

The teachers and students, collaborators and interns, funders and donors have all played a role in helping us finish this book. They should know that it is thanks to Caroline Chauncey of Harvard Education Press that the book even got started, improved along the way, and ended with wise editorial adjustments (all errors are our own!). We are profoundly grateful to her for all that she does for students and teachers through her superb work as a masterful editor.

We would like to note that all royalties from the sale of this book will go to support the Right Question Institute's work with students and teachers.

Dan Rothstein: I would like to thank my father, Benzion Rothstein (of blessed memory) and my mother, Sara Rothstein, for their lifelong precious wisdom, guidance, and encouragement, and my sisters, Ruth and Judith, for their steadfast and loving support. I am deeply grateful to the Karchmer family members and, in particular, my in-laws, Samuel and Susana Karchmer, who have been so wonderfully supportive during the long journey to this book. I have also learned so much from generations of teachers in my family: Ira and Nahara Kahn, Joseph and Phyllis Rothstein, and one who has most recently joined the ranks, Ariela Rothstein. Each of my immediate family members has contributed in special ways; my wife, Ana Karchmer, with original ideas and suggestions from the outset that have helped shape our work; my son, Nathan, with his entrepreneurial savvy that helps us think about what needs to be done next; my daughter Ariela, with her ability to connect the small and big picture that pushes us to always keep both in mind; and my daughter Talia, with her nuanced understanding of language and her valuable insights that provide a fresh student perspective from inside the classroom. They all have generously offered love, encouragement, and wise, constructive criticism that influenced my work in so many ways that I would need another book to do justice to what I have learned from them.

Luz Santana: I would like to thank Grecia Alemany and the many people who offered their insights and lessons since our beginnings in Lawrence. I would like to thank my children, Ina and Alex, for all that they have taught me. Thanks to my friends Ana Rodriguez and Roz Pastrana, Emmy Howe, Sue Kranz, and my granddaughter, Jennieke, for all their support. Special thanks to Ana Karchmer for all her work and ideas in simplifying the strategy, Pat Nelson for all her training work and for introducing me to the work of the classroom, and Stephen Quatrano for his work adapting the QFT strategy for dissemination through technology. And then, I would not have been in a position to write this book without the people who opened doors for me along the way, including Paul Opcieka, my case worker from the Welfare Department in Lawrence; Patricia Karl, from The Lawrence Youth Commission; and Mel King, from the MIT Community Fellows Program.

We both feel very fortunate to have had the chance to work with each other and with Agnes Bain for so long. We have managed to endure the very demanding challenges we've faced in order to carry out the mission of the Right Question Institute.

We continually learn from each other and we have also learned so much together about how to take the gifts of insight and wisdom we have gathered from the people with whom we have worked and share them with more people. We are profoundly grateful to the late Nancy Rodriguez and the parents in Lawrence, Massachusetts, who worked alongside her many years ago. One evening back then, early in our collaboration, Nancy was standing in front of a school committee meeting and turned to us and said: "We need more people up here who can ask questions." We're working on it, Nancy. We hope this book will do justice to your insight and the notion that important ideas for improving education for all people can come from unexpected and often overlooked sources of wisdom.

About the Authors

Dan Rothstein and Luz Santana are codirectors of The Right Question Institute, a nonprofit organization that disseminates a strategy that makes it possible for all people, no matter their educational or literacy level, to learn to advocate for themselves and participate in decisions that affect them on all levels of a democratic society.

Dan Rothstein spent many years learning from the people with whom he has worked and has applied those lessons to designing strategies to promote more effective self-advocacy and citizen participation efforts. Prior to his work with The Right Question Institute, he developed and implemented education programs in Kentucky, Massachusetts, and Israel as a community educator, organizer, and urban planner. He served as Director of Neighborhood Planning for the City of Lawrence, Massachusetts, and was a Fulbright Scholar and a National Academy of Education Spencer Fellow. He graduated from Harvard College and earned a doctorate in education and social policy from the Harvard Graduate School of Education, where he served as an editor of the *Harvard Educational Review*.

Luz Santana has modeled in her own life—raising her family on welfare, working on the factory floor, going back to school, and then sharing her new skills with others—much of what The Right Question Institute aims to accomplish through its work. Prior to her work with The Right Question Institute, Santana worked as a housing services counselor and parent advocate. She has extensive experience designing and implementing applications of the Right Question Strategy in low-income communities around the country, and is recognized nationally for the participatory trainings and workshops she has designed and facilitated. Santana was a Community Fellow at MIT. She holds a BA and master's degree from the Springfield College School of Human Services.

Index